The *Suspense* Collector's Companion

Revised and expanded 2020 edition

by Joseph W. Webb, Ph.D.

This book contains QR codes!

This book contains many links to Internet pages that have more information about a topic, or identify a source, or an audio file.

Some of those links are long and can be a chore to enter using a keyboard.

If you are using a smartphone or a tablet, download a QR code scanner app (there are many; my favorite is HP's LinkReader... just search for Linkreader in your phone's app store) and use it to quickly move to the desired Internet page or other destination without typing. It's like taking a picture of that section of the printed page.

There are many free QR apps that work very well. Your smartphone or tablet may already include the software in their operating system.

Practice using this one. It links to the page of entertainment and nostalgia researcher and author Martin Grams http://mgram1.wix.com/martingramsbooks.

This page intentionally left blank.

TABLE OF CONTENTS

continued...

TABLE OF CONTENTS,
continued

Introduction

A brief new word for this latest edition: Greetings, fellow *Suspense* fans! This effort is for you and all fans of the series, and honestly, for yours truly. The goal is to increase interest and appreciation of the series and its era. This is definitely not a history of *Suspense* with lists of episodes, casts, and plot descriptions. Those items are better left to others who have done them and will do much better jobs at those in the future. This is a compendium of curiosities that have captured my attention and deepened my affection for the series. For that reason, there is no overriding continuing narrative, so you can pick and choose any section of this book as you need it. There is another goal, and that is to provide some of the history of the collecting of radio recordings that can be used by new collectors and fans to give them context as to how we got here, with so many recordings, and to offer deep gratitude to all early collectors who saved them. Most are anonymous today, many were acquaintances and friends, now passed away. Without their generous efforts of their time and money and devotion they shared then and share now, there would be nothing to listen to, or collect!

I began collecting radio programs in the early 1970s, in high school. The most popular series that family members recalled around the Thanksgiving and Christmas tables, or those with tie-ins with comic books, were the ones I started with. Those were shows like *The Shadow,* Jack Benny's programs, *The Lone Ranger, The Green Hornet,* that were being rebroadcast or on LPs at that time during a nostalgia craze. A *Suspense* program would come to my attention now and then but would think little of it. When I began to collect in earnest (once I realized collecting comic books would be way too expensive), I started to think differently. The interest in *Suspense* grew as I heard more episodes, especially my favorites like *Three O'Clock* (March 10, 1949) and *The Crowd* (September 10, 1949). I realized that this series was quite special.

This book is a result of about 48 years of collecting radio programs. My recent collecting has been enhanced by relationships with collectors and fans of the *Suspense* history. Among them are Don Ramlow (who is working for the last two decades on a significant scholarly compendium of the series), Keith Scott (voice performer, based in Australia, who has performed worldwide, and documented the series whenever he traveled to California), Jerry Haendiges (disc expert and one of the founders of SPERDVAC), YesterdayUSA hosts and collectors Walden Hughes with John and Larry Gassman (who also were early participants in SPERDVAC), researcher John Abbott (whose books on *Yours Truly, Johnny Dollar* have set a high bar for future radio researchers).

There are many fellow travelers at the online OTR forum Cobalt Club (where we know each other with names like Nightkey, Ghemrats, Geezer, Artatoldotr, Bojim1, JBSteele, Otrhead, Emruf7, Harlow Wilcox, Dan Fielding, Tom-In-Ohio, KDMarket, Completedayman, Shadowsmom, Chasedad, Toebig, Schriever, and many others. And me? I'm Greybelt, known as the "Cobaltian Completist" when I post there. (Thanks for checking and contributing to my crazy ideas).

Other collectors like Doug Hopkinson, David Gibbs, Randy Riddle, Sammy Jones, Bob Merritt, and Travis Conner have helped guide me through the fascinating world of transcription discs. Veteran collectors have shared their collections and knowledge with me, including folks like Stu Weiss, Bob Burnham, Jerry Chapman, Frank Rosin, Bob Blume, Archie Hunter, Jeff Keil, David Oxford, Dave Lennick, Karl Schadow, Dick Judge, and many others. David Goldin's RadioGoldindex is a constant online resource for me; thank you Mr. G for making that available to all. The prolific Martin Grams, author and nostalgia event maven, built my interest in *Suspense* because of his high school project that turned out to be a marvelous reference book for the series. It's been fun meeting John C. Alsedek who keeps the flame of *Suspense* alive in new dramas and has great interest performing the missing episodes.

There are some collectors who have passed away who had positive effects on my collecting. Dave Siegel taught me how to collect series of programs and was a good good friend. Bob Burchett was generous to me when I was a young collector who thought I could do a hobby newsletter and that it should look professional. Ben Kibler taught me the ins and outs of online radio research, and Jim Beshires founded the Old Time Radio Researchers and encouraged my participation in the group.

Special acknowledgment of the staff of the Thousand Oaks Library in California is essential. It is there that the scripts for many years of *Suspense* are preserved in the KNX Collection (KNX was the CBS station where *Suspense* was produced). In June 2019, Keith Scott and I had a research visit and were generously assisted by the staff members of Jeanette Berard, Cynthia Thomas, and others who work to preserve radio history. For years I had heard of their cooperation and encouragement of researchers, and their excellent reputation is well deserved.

I know I left people out. Thanks, Annie, wife of 40 years... this is what I've been doing when I've been hiding in my office! And now that we're retired, it's what I'm doing in between items on the honey-do list when we're not out exploring this new phase of our adventure.

Joseph W. Webb, Ph.D.
July 2019

A Collector's Brief History of *Suspense*

Suspense was one of radio's greatest series, with a tenure of 20 years covering parts of three decades. An anthology, the program featured many of the most prominent Hollywood and Broadway performers, a top-notch production team, and superb direction.

As radio drama met its slow demise in favor of television, *Suspense* remained a staple of the genre through the 1950s and the early 1960s, cast with veteran radio performers of exceptional talent.

The current version of this book began as a way to document *Suspense's* missing episodes, the recordings that still elude today's old time radio enthusiasts. In the process, much information was gathered about the series, especially the backroom machinations and various trivial points of interest. I found these to be fascinating. Researching the programs we listen to enhances the enjoyment of them. Research shared among collectors also binds our hobby together in common cause and appreciation.

Research about the series is easier than ever before, with many archives of newspapers and industry magazines available online. Many of these are profiled in the research section of this book so other collectors can use them, too.

One particularly interesting topic is that of east and west coast broadcasts. There is now much better documentation about a very unique aspect of Suspense broadcasts at the beginning of Roma Wines sponsorship. It seems that CBS could not get its own networks to coordinate a common time or day when Roma Wines broadcasts could begin. For about ten months, Suspense had live broadcasts on Thursdays for the East and the Midwest, and then another live performance on Mondays.

While *Suspense* is considered a solid mainstay of the radio era, its life was actually more rocky than commonly believed. It had a troubled history, was nearly canceled in 1947, had a disastrous (and thankfully short) hour-long format in early 1948, and seemed on the verge of cancellation for much of the late 1950s.

The show had big budgets in the 1940s to pay the big stars, best writers and technicians, and a full orchestra with musicians of the highest caliber. The 1950s radio series saw their budgets cut and shifted to television. *Suspense* survived. Because the series was an anthology, they were able to shift from big Hollywood stars to other movie performers and some extraordinary radio performers who were mostly anonymous in public. There were no stars under contract to play the leads in every episode, so its stories and casts changed every week. That made its costs lower than character-based dramas and comedies. The show's long tenure also meant that it could take advantage of an audience that was changing and turning over to re-present its scripts and those of other similar programs (such as *Escape, Romance* and others) from earlier years. It's not a repeat if you never heard it before. And if *Suspense* repeated it, that usually meant it was a darned good script since they had hundreds to choose from. A repeat meant the chance it could be savored once more.

The show persisted until that day of September 30, 1962, known among collectors as the "day radio drama died," when *Suspense* and *Yours Truly, Johnny Dollar* had their final broadcasts.

How Radio Fans Saved Suspense

The fact that so many *Suspense* episodes survived is a story in itself. It's easy to understand how recordings of big sponsored network productions produced in Hollywood, starting with the Roma Wines run and concluding with Auto-Lite would survive. It's surprising there are any missing from that period at all, but a small number are not available. Networks, stations, actors and agents, and ad agencies often had transcription disc recordings made for their use. Archive copies or duplicate discs would be made available for the Armed Forces Radio Service so they could broadcast for their network, worldwide. Because of all of those recording sources, most everything survived in at least one recorded format or another.

After Auto-Lite's tenure ended, and lacking a replacement sponsor, the risk of losing episode recordings increased. There were no advertisers or others that needed extra copies for their business or archival use.

In late 1956, *Suspense* production shifted to recording tape instead of transcription discs. This had great benefits in production and editing. Transcription discs could be used only once. Recording tape could be used multiple times. It is likely that CBS kept a library of recorded tapes in an archive, but the informal preservation of the series, such as radio stations recording the network feeds for later broadcast that day or soon thereafter, disappeared. They had no incentive to store the tapes after they served their purpose, so they reused them. This was an option that they did not have with transcription discs. They could erase history, and save money in the process. Transcriptions would eventually be thrown out; radio fans often saved the dumpster-bound treasures out of curiosity and eventually with interest in preservation of the golden era.

On the positive side, home tape recorders became more affordable and more numerous. These taped recordings made by 1950s and 1960s radio fans saved the day, and grew more critical for the preservation of the series. Those home recordists had no clue how important their contributions would be to today's fans and to archivists. For this portion of the series run, there are many episodes where the home recordings are the only ones that survive, especially for the years 1960 to 1962. These supplement the few official network recordings that exist as well as those saved by the Armed Forces Radio Service.

Regarding AFRS, collectors have heard more than once that many of these discs were systematically destroyed. They were supposed to be, but many service and radio personnel saved these, too. One long-time collector learned about discs in a warehouse and was refused access to them and chided him in the harshest way for even asking about them. The discs were being destroyed by using them for rifle target practice! (More about the critical importance of AFRS recordings in saving *Suspense* later).

Just as a comparison to today's recording methods and how technological advances have changed them, all one has to look at is the cost of recording tape. This offers a perspective about how those home recordists really had to make an investment to record programs and keep them. The temptation to keep recording over things they did not want to keep was tremendous. A little "round number" arithmetic illustrates what they went through, and how lucky we are today in terms of recording costs.

Consider this:

- In the late 1950s, recording tape cost about $1.50 for 30 minutes of recording time. That's about $13.75 in today's dollars.

- A 1 terabyte external hard drive costs about $75.00. Using the size of a typical mp3 format file (at 128kps) you could store over 33,000 recordings. The cost per half hour recording is $0.0022!

- That means that the cost of storing a half hour recording has *fallen* by 6,000 times!

Put it more simply in very rough terms: for the same inflation-adjusted price you could store 6 programs in 1950 you can now store 33,000! This is an amazing time to be a collector of old time radio recordings.

And think of this: storing 33,000 recordings in the tape format most used in the 1970s (quarter-track on 1800′ reels) would require about *one ton* of recording tape while a 1TB drive may weigh about 6 ounces! That's about 1/5300th the weight!

Why Suspense *is Really Good...* *Most All of the Time*

There are certain periods of the *Suspense* twenty-year run that are better than others, but the show always had excellent production values compared to others of its time. The anthology format allowed each episode to be unique and for its producers and actors to ply and explore their craft without worrying about week-to-week continuity.

The weekly Hollywood stars added a dimension that was different from other "star" series like *Lux Radio Theatre* and others. *Lux* had actors in roles that were familiar to them, usually adapting the motion picture that the public recognized them for.

Suspense often cast guest stars against type, putting comedians in dramatic roles, or actors associated with criminal "tough guys" playing sentimental softies. That style of casting was very attractive to actors who wanted to break from their type-casting, even for just one night, which often resulted in an interesting and enthusiastic performance. A successful *Suspense* engagement could lead to a wider range of roles in the future.

The thirty minute format of *Suspense* also helped. In *Lux*, the actors were often portraying characters as they had in the original movies, and listeners accepted their work because they happy to hear the stars they saw on screen. *Suspense* was a different matter.

Some movie stars were not skilled at the craft of radio acting, where their voice had to carry all of a scene's subtleties. That was an occasional problem, but the scripts for *Suspense* were usually top-notch, selected for the skill level and talent of the actor, with action that moved at a quick pace. Combined with the excellent regular cast members and the extraordinary background music that supported the emotions of each scripted moment, the shortcomings of the non-radio pros were usually less of an issue. If the guest actor could not deliver a nuanced performance, the originally composed musical bridges often carried the sentiment and the actor went along for the ride.

Collecting Suspense in the Digital Era

My ardent collection of this series in digital form began in 2004, but I collected the series for many years before on reels and cassettes. Collecting in digital formats is much more convenient than tape formats in the 1970s and 1980s. I remember being frustrated at that time by finding better quality recordings of individual episodes but not having an easy way of inserting them into my collection and keeping maintaining broadcast date order.

Today, it's easy to fix problems and replace shows because of computers and very easy file management procedures. But the old ways of collecting still haunt some collections. Many of the episodes in circulation still have incorrect labeling problems that originated years ago. Of course they do: many collections just converted the audio tape recordings into digital recordings, and collectors based their file names on incorrect information from cassette labels or reel contents sheets.

There were many missing episodes of *Suspense*, and collectors wanted to note that fact and also make space for them in their collections by using "placeholders" that were other recordings.

This was a problem. Truly missing shows were replaced by copies of performances from other dates. The "pretender" recordings were put there by innocent ignorance, but also they may have been with the intent of putting the right one in if it ever appeared. Those intentions may never have been acted on, so early digital collections of the series frequently had these errors. Many reel and cassette collections were digitized to the mp3 file format starting in the 1990s, with these errors and more.

Today, we can just delete those bad files when we find them.

These problems reflected the lack of information resources available during that period in the hobby. The were errors of well-intentioned hobbyists. They did not have access to information like we do today, especially the resources of search engines like Google and data bases. Thankfully, many of these badly constructed collections have fallen out of circulation and have been replaced by more accurate sets assembled by more attentive collectors.

While this is a splendid result of the hard work of today's collectors and fans, there is a downside to it. Those older collections fell by the wayside even though they may have had individual recordings of great value. As the old saying goes, the baby was being thrown out with the bathwater.

Where are Those Missing Suspense Shows?

Thankfully, through the dedication of collectors, most all of the *Suspense* series exists and is available to fans and researchers. In 2019, it appears that there are 34 missing recordings with 14 one-time performances and 20 that had additional performances.

The 14 single-performance episodes have the highest priority to find.

The count of missing programs has decreased in recent years. Collaborative research by some ardent *Suspense* fans, including yours truly, and generous assistance of collectors who are aware of our work, has helped greatly.

The most recent change is that the missing version of 1957-09-15 *Night on Red Mountain* appeared in mid-2018 in *two different* AFRS recordings.

This is the current list of the 14 missing single-performance episodes:

DATE	TITLE
1942-07-01	Life of Nellie James
1942-07-08	Rope
1942-07-15	Westbound Limited
1943-02-09	The Hangman Won't Wait (first half of show exists)
1943-02-23	Will You Walk into My Parlor? (first half of show exists)
1943-03-09	The Phantom Archer
1945-07-26	Fury and Sound (AFRS transcription sold on eBay)
1946-02-28	The Keenest Edge
1948-07-08	The Last Chance
1950-06-15	Deadline
1951-11-12	Mission of the Betta
1951-11-19	The Embezzler
1956-01-03	The Eavesdropper
1956-08-01	Massacre at the Little Big Horn

Three of the fourteen shows are from the opening summer 1942 programs, when it was produced in New York as a Summer series. It is likely these are lost forever. They might not have been recorded.

Some of that might be a cultural issue: the difference between radio work in New York and Hollywood. When you examine the existing recordings in the hobby of preserving golden age of radio recordings, it is obvious that most of the shows in circulation are Hollywood productions. Not all of this is by chance. There was a loss of many transcriptions in a warehouse fire in the New York area, decades ago, which is tragic. There is another factor, that cultural one.

Early in my collecting I was able to meet many radio actors and technicians from New York. The way one of them explained it to me was rather simple: radio in New York was work, radio in Hollywood was art. In New York in the early 1940s, it was believed that there was little reason in broadcasting that the shows would have an audience again. Live radio was just fine, and that's what people wanted. The actors moved from studio to studio, sometimes running across town or giving a cabbie a big tip to rush them to their next gig. Someone would hand them a script, they'd scan it, and off they'd go. When it was done, they'd rush to their next assignment. Soap operas in the morning, kid's shows in the afternoon, big dramas and comedies at night. The big evening-time shows would get more preparation because of the bigger audiences and bigger budgets. But rarely were actors having their performances recorded unless they needed a recording to get a job, or create a portfolio, or the network needed a recording to attract a sponsor.

Suspense was just an unremarkable summer 1942 replacement series in the minds of many. There was little fanfare around it, making it plausible to assert that *shows of that summer may never have been recorded*.

On the opposite coast, however, there was greater interest in recording the radio programs from an art perspective, but there was also a practical aspect in the movie business that many films would be released again, beyond an initial theater run. It is likely that this sensibility of Hollywood entertainment culture affected the decisions to record radio programs. Remember: at that time there was no such thing as television broadcast of movies, cable channels, video tapes or DVDs, or Netflix, meaning that the only way to see a favorite movie again was to hope it would be re-released into the theaters.

There was also the aspect of being in a time zone that was three hours later than New York. It was common for high profile programs to have two performances, one for the East Coast, and another for the West Coast. That did not always fit the needs of individual stations. Some might record from network feeds on transcriptions and use those recordings to play for Pacific or Mountain Time Zone at a better time for their listeners. It was not common to use transcriptions for playback of network programs until the late 1940s. Individual stations would play transcriptions, especially syndicated shows, since the 1930s. Syndicated programs were designed for playback, while network broadcasts were not.

Suspense as "just another radio series" was be the common sentiment until the show moved to Hollywood in early 1943. The real catalyst for *Suspense* to achieve prominence would be the performance of *Sorry, Wrong Number,* but that was months away.

The next cluster of programs are two missing single-performances from November 1951 and four multiple performances of the same year. The network transcriptions may have been pulled from a shelf and never returned to their rightful place. The best hope for those episodes is that AFRS recordings of them surface.

Two missing programs are known to exist as AFRS transcriptions, sold on eBay, but are not circulating among collectors at this time. We have other documentation of them in terms of scripts and newspaper listings, and also a short story adaptation.

Luckily, some *Suspense* scripts were used in other US series (such as CBS' *Escape* and *Romance*) or in the UK (*Appointment with Fear*) and Australia (*Tension*). Some new recreations (American Radio Theater, Blue Hours Productions) are available, so we can at least hear them as radio plays and not just as scripts to read. Recordings of these productions are available online, and links to them are provided in these listings.

There are still stacks of AFRS transcriptions around the world that have yet to be found but might be in record shops, warehouses, record collections, and other places. Some of the missing *Suspense* may be sitting silently there.

Collecting the Many Variations of Suspense

In 2004, I began to collect *Suspense* in digital formats, and began to search for the best recordings. Thinking that there might be one or two recordings of each episode (network and possibly an AFRS recording), I was surprised to find that there were many other types of *Suspense* recordings available.

I now am committed, along with the many collectors who help me, to collect all episode versions that can be found, including broadcasts, rehearsals, network, AFRS/AFRTS, broadcast airchecks, home recordings, East and West Coast performances, and others, whatever those recordings might be. For this reason, I am called a "completist." I wear the name with pride, an am happy to share it with others.

Sorry, Wrong Number, for example, was such a memorable and successful broadcast it was performed many times in *Suspense* history, and was also released as a record set by Decca for home listening, three different times. There was even a BBC production of the script in 1948, and another in 1949.

Upgrades and different versions of shows are still being found.

For example, three different network versions of *August Heat* from the same date exist, each with unique show openings ("Now... Roma Wines, R-O-M-A...," "The Roma Wine Company of Fresno, California...," and finally "Now... The Roma Wine Company of Fresno, California..."). Is one just a clipped opening? Or are there three distinct recordings for this date? Is one a rehearsal? Are these East and West coast recordings? There are still mysteries that we may never solve.

A missing version of *Donovan's Brain*, part one, appeared recently when a collector found a commercially released cassette from the 1970s. It turned out to be the missing East Coast broadcast from the period when *Suspense* aired on Thursdays for East and Central time zones and on Mondays for Mountain and Pacific time zones. The recording was right under the noses of old time radio hobbyists for decades. (The twice-a-week Roma period is detailed in a separate chapter). There are also airchecks available of the story's two parts available.

There are many airchecks recorded by performers or advertisers, or even radio stations, that have been identified. The aforementioned home tape recordings have bits of news, local commercials, or other items from their local station. This lets us hear how radio sounded to listeners of that time.

As I began research about the series to verify dates of the recordings, I found much more. *Suspense* had a fascinating behind-the-scenes story that was mostly untold. Therefore, I am always looking for newspaper and magazine clippings, broadcast industry articles, and script cover pages for as many of the programs as possible.

The Crucial Role of Armed Forces Radio in Preserving Suspense

The radio networks made their network programs available to the Armed Forces Radio Service (AFRS) as part of the wartime effort. In fact, the first producer of *Suspense*, Charles Vanda, left the CBS network to help lead the establishment of the AFRS organization.

Suspense was popular on AFRS from the beginning. It was featured there for most of all of its twenty year broadcast history. Recordings of the series was a staple of AFRS for more than twenty years after it went off the air. Because AFRS kept releasing recordings, the plentiful amount of discs made it possible for the series to survive. There are many episodes for which the only copies that exist are AFRS recordings. Most of the missing shows that have been found in the last decade have been from AFRS transcriptions.

AFRS (and later AFRTS when they added television services) made the most of *Suspense* in its program offerings. *Suspense* was released many times through the decades, usually under its own series title, with advertiser and sponsor commercials and CBS references edited out, as was their required practice.

Through the 1970s, radio drama was an important for of entertainment for US armed forces personnel assigned to locations that still had no television access. "Old time radio show" rebroadcasts also entertained their families.

AFRS released *Suspense* programs and other programs in multiple formats. Sometimes edited programs would be part of *AFRTS Adventure Theater* or *AFRTS Mystery Theater*. The strangest sounding AFRTS releases are from the late 1970s and early 1980s. These *Suspense* episodes are a hodgepodge of show elements. They have pieces of openings and closings from every *Suspense* era, cobbled together as one in a Frankenstein-like edit. These were new openings and closings patched onto the body of the drama. In these versions, episode names and casts were usually edited out to make them sound "newer" (since many of the prominent Hollywood *Suspense* actors had passed away).

These badly edited programs are actually disturbing to listen to for OTR purists, but may be the only format in which some of the missing shows might be found. At the time of this writing, these odd versions have not yielded a missing program, but supplement the network and AFRS copies that already exist. (The strangest AFRS packaging has a *Suspense* drama with the opening and closing of *Inner Sanctum*!).

AFRS employed a numbering system of their transcriptions that can help collectors to identify if they may have a missing program on them. The numbering generally works on programs in the 1940s. Transcription collector Randy Riddle has posted instructions to determine if a collector has stumbled upon one of the missing shows as an AFRS transcription. AFRS transcriptions have a label, just like LP records do, that identify the series. They do not list the episode title, but have a show number "rubber stamped" onto the label. The dating method that Mr. Riddle details are usually accurate for the 1940s and early 1950s AFRS recordings. In the late 1950s, the program numbering is often haphazard. His instructions are on his website and can be found at http://randsesotericotr.podbean.com/do-you-have-a-lost-episode-of-suspense/

After those years, AFRS had multiple releases of the series with different numbering schemes that did not always follow original network broadcast order. This fact sometimes led to misdating of many series, such as many sets of the fine CBS police series, *The Line-Up*. The collectors who recorded *Line-Up* shows from the AFRS discs assumed that the AFRS numbering exactly followed the original broadcast dates. It was not until researcher Stewart Wright compiled a log of the series from the scripts stored at the Thousand Oaks Library in California that the shows could be identified properly. He matched the script dialog with the recordings to do so. Until then, *The Line-Up* collections were absolute messes.

Depending on the year that an AFRS transcription was pressed, there may be information etched in the smooth or blank area around the label. Sometimes this has the date of the original broadcast and the name of the episode. In later AFRTS releases, the etched information relates to internal information that has no real meaning today, but those numbers should still be recorded as there are AFRS/AFRTS specialists who know how to decipher them.

I maintain an online spreadsheet of AFRS program numbers for their releases of *Suspense*. The address is https://docs.google.com/spreadsheets/d/1Dwt CgHCHkrPniy9UklqaAGu_8EOAz2pm4gUe MPk8Po4/edit?usp=sharing

In 2016, I interviewed Mr. Riddle about his efforts to collect transcription recordings. A recording can be streamed at his site http://randsesotericotr.podbean.com/e/intervi ew-by-joe-web-11-20-2016/.

Collectors Did Not Always Hold AFRS Recordings in High Regard: Now We Do

In the early years of collecting old radio programs, many collectors believed that AFRS[1] programs were "inferior" to network recordings since they were not the full recordings as broadcast. AFRS recordings did not have commercials, and there were times when some portions of the programs such as the announcement of the next week's episode or the name of the program following in the next few minutes were edited out.

A program like *Fred Allen* was so packed with topical information and ad-lib jokes about current events that it could lose relevance by the time the AFRS audience would hear them. They would not have the context to understand the references. This is one reason why there are very few *Fred Allen* recordings in AFRS formats. This was not an issue for *Suspense* but the editors occasionally removed dialog to fit the broadcast time allotted, especially in the re-releases in the 1970s and 1980s. Sometimes the AFRS production personnel would speed up the body of the program to make it fit into the required time. (Some of the AFRTS western *Sagebrush Theater* releases of *Fort Laramie* and others were sped up significantly, and it is strange to hear them).

Early collectors made the characteristics of AFRS recordings worse, but they should be forgiven. Because reel-to-reel recording tape was expensive, many tape recordings of AFRS programs were cut by collectors at the end of the drama, eliminating the AFRS announcements and filler music, and saving money by being able to fit more shows onto their tape

1 Please note that when we refer to AFRS we also include AFRTS, its name after television service began.

reels. There were many 1800' quarter-track reels of Suspense that had 16 episodes rather than the usual 12 that were extremely popular among collectors. This listing is from a very popular reel that collectors could buy from the dealer *Golden Age Radio*, a very popular program source in the 1970s.

```
REEL RP-222 - SUSPENSE (A)
1-L  "The Wait" with Maria Palmer and John Dehner - 9/7/58 - Revolutionary leader
     "The Stool Pigeon" with John Dehner - 9/20/55 - Betrayal on Devils' Island
     "Two Platinum Capsules" - 1/10/56? - Boys with death in their pocket
     "Classified Secret" with Parley Baer - 11/22/55 - Cross country bus
2-L  "A Story of Poison" with Joseph Kearns - 9/13/55 - A notorious murderer
     "Game Hunt" with Raymond Lawrence - 4/3/56 - Safari in Africa
     "The Lonely Heart" with Ben Wright - 4/10/56 - A missing body
     "The Treasure Chest of Don Jose" with Raymond Burr - 10/12/58 - Buried chest
1-R  "Hollywood Hostages" with Eve McVey - 2/21/56 - Practical joke that wasn't
     "For Old Time Sake" with John Lund - 12/7/58 - A good man with a past
     "A Statement of Fact" with Cathy Lewis - 11/27/58 - Love nest murder
     "Tom Dooley" with Robert Horton - 11/30/58 - Celebrated murderer [1t.x-talk]
2-R  "A Friend of Daddy's" with Frank Lovejoy - 5/17/59 - Psychopathic war buddy
     "Spoils for Victor" with Robert Horton - 5/24/59 - Poor boy, rich girl
     "Remember Me?" with Jackie Cooper - 8/24/58 - Murderer meets old classmate
     "Goodbye, Miss Lizzie Bordon" with Paula Winslowe - 10/4/55 - Famous case
```

AFRS recordings did not include network commercials, but often replaced them with military service announcements for service personnel and families about benefits or stories of military history or other topics. These announcements were often removed by early collectors, sometimes with sloppy results.

Some "fixed" recordings were made with the best intentions by service personnel in their homes as they recorded off the air from their AFRS stations. You can understand that these service personnel were very sensitive to the costs of home recording, and were not really interested in preserving the military service announcements. These are particularly obvious in many of the surviving *Yours Truly, Johnny Dollar* recordings from the late 1950s and early 1960s.

Other collectors, believing that AFRS programs were inferior, still appreciated the fact that they had the core recordings of the drama portions. Some attempted to re-assemble network elements around the AFRS recording. They used clips of network episodes to "restore" what AFRS engineers had taken away, usually with disastrous playback results. The nature of the sound quality did not always match, so the edits were obvious. Editing skills and the right materials were usually reserved for trained production engineers, and these were not available to most collectors. They would create mistakes such as adding incorrect cast announcements (this is common in many of the home-recorded *Gunsmoke* episodes from the late 1950s as well as some episodes of *Yours Truly, Johnny Dollar*. Many of the *YTJD* recordings with this problem are identified by John Abbott in his excellent book about the series).

Today's digital audio tools are far more powerful and inexpensive, and amateurs can use them with some competence if they attempted to make the same kinds of "restoration" efforts. But there is greater respect for the AFRS recordings now, so collectors leave them intact.

Thankfully, despite the recording abuse that AFRS versions of *Suspense* have taken in collecting's early years, many of the full unblemished AFRS recordings have been found and have replaced those badly edited ones with vastly superior sound. There is now greater appreciation about the importance of AFRS recordings in preserving the history of the radio drama. Considering the equipment they had and the time pressures they were under, AFRS production engineers should be commended, and their work should be rightly considered as heroic in preserving *Suspense.*

AFRTS still plays an important worldwide role for US military and their families. The website *AFRTS Archive*, http://afrtsarchive.blogspot.com/, published by former AFRTS engineer Thom Whetston is highly recommended.

Thom served in the 1970s in Korea and Panama, but he often posts information and recordings from throughout AFRS history. He has been a great friend to the OTR hobby.

Messing with the Missing: Making Sure File Names Have Correct Dates Using Clues in the Shows

In recent years, collectors and groups like *The Old Time Radio Researchers* have made significant progress in standardizing audio file names for episodes of *Suspense* and other radio series. Today's digital collectors have benefited from these efforts. Collectors from the tape and cassette era did not have such support. Many of those collections had serious problems with file naming consistency and accuracy. When those collections were first digitized in the mid-1990s, those errors were replicated. Some of the errors were from bad handwriting in the reel contents sheets or lack of space on cassette labels. Other data were guessed or missing.

Because these older reel collections can have episode versions that have fallen out of circulation or higher sound quality because they were from disc recordings of their time, it is important to be aware of ways of detecting and correcting episode information errors.

Most of the mistitled and misdated files are obvious upon careful listening for cast names and advertisers. Yes, you can learn a lot just by listening!

An indication is that the recording has a star in the leading role that does not match that of the correctly documented performance. For example, a commonly mislabled recording that purported to be a missing episode was *Night on Red Mountain* from September 15, 1957 starring Richard Crenna. These usually turn out to be mislabeled copies of the November 20, 1960 version with Mandel Kramer.

This episode has since been found, but this is still a good example of what to listen for in the identification process because there are multiple errors. What are some of the other clues that this was a mislabeled show?

In 1957, the show was still produced in Hollywood, but in 1960 it was produced in New York.

The players in New York are quite different from the actors used in Hollywood. After a while you get to know who's where. Mandel Kramer was a very successful New York actor. Crenna was a Hollywood actor. After listening to a few shows, you get to know which actors are usually in each city.

Other misdated shows can be correctly identified by matching up advertisers or announcements for that date. Sometimes there are references to upcoming or past events, such as that week's star's upcoming movie release, making the misdating errors obvious, and giving clues to the accurate broadcast date. A quick check of the Internet Movie Data Base (www.imdb.com) can help in these cases.

Advertiser Clues: Dating Suspense *episodes using sponsorship information*

The first *Suspense* program was aired June 17, 1942 and the final episode was September 30, 1962. That was also the date of the final *Yours Truly, Johnny Dollar* broadcast, and is sometimes referred to as "the day radio drama died." *Suspense* was planned to cease production in 1961, but got a reprieve. The final 1962 show makes no mention of its cancellation. Perhaps it was believed there was a chance for a reprieve like they had in 1961.

The dates that Roma Wine and Auto-Lite sponsored the show are as follows:

- *First Roma Wines episode:*
  December 12, 1943 *The Black Curtain* with Cary Grant
- *Last Roma Wines episode:*
  November 11, 1947 *One Hundred in the Dark*
- *First Auto-Lite episode:*
  July 7, 1948 *The Last Chance* with Cary Grant *(missing)*
- *First circulating Auto-Lite episode:*
  July 15, 1948 with Ida Lupino
- *Final Auto-Lite episode:*
  June 7, 1954 *Terribly Strange Bed* with Peter Lawford

Other times in its 20-year run *Suspense* was a sustained program or had local or mixed national advertising. Over the years, there have been many misdated recordings among collectors, which could have been easily corrected because the advertiser in the recording did not match the actual dates of their sponsorship. There are shows, like *Sorry, Wrong Number*, that were repeated many times, and had the two major sponsors and were also done during the unsponsored periods.

Producer Clues: Dating Suspense Episodes by Who Was in Charge

Suspense had many producers and knowing that can help listeners place recordings into their proper era.

These are the various producers the series had, and most of them brought a special flair to the series. Others were keeping the show going at its high level of performance until the next long-tenured era began. This is the list of producers; please note there were slight deviations for vacations and other reasons in the time periods mentioned.

- **Charles Vanda**, June 1942, and two episodes in October 1945: the first producer of the series who moved to the founding staff of AFRS after leaving CBS.

- **William Spier**, July 1942- February 7, 1948, who became a celebrity star as a producer: his final production in the "mess" of the 60-minute episodes was *Donovan's Brain*. His career was also notable for *Columbia Workshop*, *Sam Spade* (for CBS and NBC), and *Philip Morris Playhouse*.

- **Robert Montgomery,** February 14, 1948 to March 26, 1948, in the ill-fated 60-minute episodes: this movie star was the wrong prescription for the maladies the series was suffering. Many of the industry publications at the time implied he was producer "in name only" as CBS was trying to make *Suspense* more "Lux-like" in its hour-long format. His relationship with the network was not good, and the confusion was a contributing factor in Spier's departure.

- **Anton M. Leader**, April 3, 1948 to June 30, 1949: filled in at the end of the 60-minute episodes, and then ushered in the Auto-Lite sponsorship with a re-vamped series. He was also known for *Words at War, Eternal Light, The Whisper Men*, and *Murder at Midnight*. His leadership does not get as much acknowledgment as it deserves because his time in the position was relatively short.

- **William Spier** returned for another year beginning September 1, 1949 and ending June 29, 1950.

- **Robert Stevens** filled in for Spier on for some episodes in Fall 1949. This was likely for "training" for his direction of 105 of the 206 episodes of the *Suspense* television series.

- **Elliott Lewis**, one of radio's most amazing talents as a producer, director, writer, dramatic and comedy actor had the show from August 31, 1950 to July 20, 1954. He worked on *Suspense* as an actor beginning in the mid-1940s. His credits included *Broadway Is My Beat, Crime Classics, On Stage*, and *Phil Harris and Alice Faye* where he played Remley, one of the funniest characters ever in radio comedy. With the competition of television, Lewis used his *Suspense* time to occasionally experiment with the radio medium. One of those experimental themes was more topical programs which might fit the phrase "ripped from headlines," which is a common approach to television, even today. His *Suspense* work was often uneven, unfortunately, one of the downsides of pushing the boundaries, but there were enough episodes of high and thoughtful quality that he is held in high regard. His work on other series, however, had greater impact and was more memorable.

- **Norman Macdonnell**, July 27, 1954 to December 16, 1954, best known for his producing of *Escape* and many other CBS shows such as *The Adventures of Philip Marlowe* in the early 1950s "silver age" of radio. He directed *Suspense* during Spier's 1949-1950 return as producer. Macdonnell is especially respected because of his superb work on *Gunsmoke* for most every episode of its run. Between *Escape* and the sometimes similar *Romance*, he was well-familiar with the *Suspense* franchise and had a very good, but very brief time, as the show's producer. It is possible that the expiration of the Auto-Lite sponsorship led to Elliott Lewis' departure and that Macdonnell's *Suspense* tenure was always intended to be short-lived. His television work included *The Virginian* and *Gunsmoke*.

- **Antony Ellis**, December 23, 1954 to October 16, 1956: Ellis was also an actor, director, producer, and writer. He was an exceptional talent. Ellis was involved with the series *Romance*. Many collectors adore his late 1950s series *Frontier Gentleman*.

- **William N. Robson**, October 23, 1956 to August 23, 1959: Bill Robson was a radio powerhouse as a producer, director, and writer. By the time he got to *Suspense*, the series had no sponsor, tight budgets, and no longer sought the presence of big Hollywood stars. No matter: the cadre of CBS radio actors at his disposal carried the day with fine productions. More than half of the Robson productions used scripts from earlier in the series, *Escape*, and others. He held the series together as radio dramas were being canceled all around him. Robson had an exceptional career dating back to the mid-1930s. They included *Calling All Cars, Columbia Workshop, Man Behind the Gun, Request Performance, Escape, Pursuit, Romance, CBS Radio Workshop,* and the westerns *Luke Slaughter,* and *Have Gun Will Travel.*

The series moved back to New York at end of August 1959 and no longer had high-profile producers. Their productions were more pedestrian in nature, without had the high visibility leadership that began with Spier. The New York productions are not bad, they are worth listening to, but they are not always as inspired. There were many repeat performances as well as re-writes of some *The Mysterious Traveler* scripts at this time.

- **Paul Roberts**, August 30, 1959 to November 27, 1960: Roberts was the first of the New York producers who took over the program. He had previously worked on late 1950s series such as *CBS Radio Workshop, Indictment,* and soap operas.

- **Bruno Zirato, Jr.**, June 25, 1961 to May 27, 1962: Zirato worked on the early New York run of *Broadway is My Beat* (before it went to Hollywood where the show realized its full potential), *Stagestruck,* and *Yours Truly Johnny Dollar.* Zirato's greatest success, however, came from his production of television game shows such as *I've Got a Secret.*

- **Fred Hendrickson**, June 3, 1962 to Sept 30, 1962: Hendrickson produced the final season of *Suspense.* His radio experience included *Let's Pretend,* and *Yours Truly Johnny Dollar.*

Recording Technology and Collector Habits Affected the Accuracy of Early Collections

Some of the dating problems were introduced by misguided good intentions. As some of early collectors assembled their reel-to-reel tape sets of *Suspense,* they encountered many situations where episodes were missing. They hoped they would eventually appear.

Since the primary form of collecting in that early era was 1800' reels, each track of the four tracks on the reel held 90 minutes of programming at 3.75 inches per second. Many collectors timed out how much tape would pass to create a silent period in the tape where they could eventually insert the recording of a missing show so they could keep episodes in date order.

An example of this is from the collection of deceased collector Gary Husa, who donated his reels to the University of North Texas. Details about the collection can be viewed at their website http://findingaids.library.unt.edu/?p=collections/controlcard&id=288.

Item 27 is a reel content sheet that has a run of *Suspense* dates that includes missing programs from November 1951. The archivists charge a fee for copying a recording, but they did send me a copy of the reel's contents sheet at no charge. The recording fee would be assessed even if Mr. Husa had left a blank spot; the fee was for an archivist to locate the reel, mount it, and listen, so getting the contents sheet first made sense.

SUSPENSE

1L   11/5/51   The Trials of Thomas Shaw
       11/12/51   Mission of the Bells
       11/19/51   The Embezzler

2L   11/26/51   A Misfortune in Pearls
  375-797   12/3/51   A Murderous Revision
  807-1420   12/10/51   Blackjack to Kill

1R   5-347   12/17/51   The Case History of a Gambler
       12/24/51   The Night Before Christmas
  800-1387   12/31/51   Rogue Male

2R   5-348   3/17/52   The Wreck of the Old 97
       10sec dropout 3/4 way thru

RESTRICTED· ship 2/9/79
360-757   12/8/52   Joker Wild

It was clear from the handwritten notes on the sheet that Husa followed this pattern of collecting, with spaces for the programs left on the reel, but the episodes were not there. Note that there were tape counter notations for the shows that were on the reel, but no such notations for the shows that were not. Why? If the shows were there, the counter figures would be known and written down.

Other collectors created another well-intentioned problem. If a missing episode had a repeat performance somewhere in the *Suspense* run, they would insert that existing performance from a different year (and likely a different cast) as a placeholder until the correct recording surfaced.

This practice that led to many misdated and out of order programs because the notes documenting each reel of tape would not always be sent to each collector. Those notes also disappeared when the reel collections were encoded to digital formats in the 1990s.

The fact that so many of the reel content sheets were handwritten – computers were not yet a household appliance – meant that sloppy handwriting or shorthand notes could lead to errors. Many times collectors did not have access to copiers so they hand wrote new content sheets for reels they would trade to other collectors.

Collecting on reels often created yet more challenges. It was common at that time to arrange trades of recordings on an hour for hour basis, meaning that they were collecting by individual shows. Today's collectors have been spoiled, in a sense, by being able to get long runs of series all in one set. It was not that way in the 1960s and 1970s. Collectors were finding discs in numerous places, and sought other collectors who were doing the same thing, and then exchanging recordings. Recording was expensive, for the equipment first, and also for the supplies.

Every time you made a copy, you added defects to the recordings, even if you were a skilled recordist. Each generation of recordings added additional "tape hiss," a background noise that built up as each collector made copies for others who in turn made copies for others. Collectors would make efforts to get trading contacts who had a reputation for getting shows that were "close to source" such as copies of disc recordings or were no more than two or three generations away from the original disc recording.

Other times, the lack of good show logs, or just plain sloppiness, compounded the problems of misdated shows. There were many collections that did not track show dates, just show titles alone. Not everyone was interested in archival accuracy, they just wanted to hear the shows. That's fine, but when those collections would be shared with others over the years, the inaccuracies were being shared with them, and perpetuated.

In the months of preparation of this latest revision of this book, I had the privilege of working with a few older collections of *Suspense* and other programs that were on reel. There have been many poor-sounding episodes of this series in circulation, especially from its later years. Many of those were "fixed" by collectors through the years to remove hiss and hum and other problems. Every few years another collector would try their hand at improving the sound of these recordings. In some cases, they made the recordings worse because of the digital encoding process that can leave artifacts of compression that are especially evident in quiet passages. By working with reels of collectors from the early 1970s, it was clear that many of these episodes were in bad sound even in that time. But they were fresh and had never been "fixed" which meant that modern audio software, within the cost reach of most every collector, could start clean, and improve the audio without compounding problems and the artifacts of encoding. Some of these had marked improvement over the commonly circulating copies. It was worth the time to seek out these collections and to spend the hours needed to improve the recordings.

This is a marvelous time to be working on a project for any series, not just *Suspense*. Today's collectors have vast information resources that early collectors did not have, and even a small amount of diligence in research is big compared to what could be done when the hobby was in its infancy. Because programs are in digital format, making copies does not change the sound.

In the end, nothing beats listening to the programs for clues about dates and other episode characteristics. Knowing the beginning dates of advertiser sponsorship, the dates when certain directors and producers worked on the program, which announcers were used, and other important characteristics. This makes the screening process of looking for missing shows and different versions better and more accurate.

Collector Resources

There are two excellent resources to check common *Suspense* episode identification errors. One is at http://sites.google.com/site/otrerrors/s-errors/suspense-errors.

 This site is maintained by collector Andrew Steinberg, who has posted previous versions of this document for the site, as well as his own notes about misdated recordings. Many of the misdated recordings have dropped out of circulation because of the research work of the Old Time Radio Researchers, which documents proper dates of programs and creates sets of recordings that are generally free of these issues. Mr. Steinberg is an active member of the organization.

Another site has not been updated for more than 10 years, but identifies missing shows and brief details about them. Some of the shows noted as missing have been discovered since the site was created. http://www.usfamily.net/web/wpattinson/otr/suspense/suslost.shtml.

Many attempts to contact the site owner have failed.

Books About Suspense

There are two books about the series. *Suspense: Twenty Years of Thrills and Chills* by Martin Grams, Jr. is available from amazon.com. Mr. Grams wrote the book as a high school project many years ago. Its best part is a complete log with descriptions and casts for virtually every episode.

 Since it was first published, some missing programs have been found and some new research materials have surfaced. Mr. Grams has not updated the book contents but has had the book reprinted as it was originally published. It is highly recommended.

Another is *Suspense* by Darryl Shelton, available from Bear Manor Media http://www.bearmanormedia.com/suspen se-the-radio-program-television-program-comics-and-mystery-magazines-by-darryl-shelton?filter_name=shelton.

The book is also available through amazon.com. The Shelton book includes a short story that originally appeared in *Suspense Magazine* that was adapted from the script of a missing show, and also includes a script of a missing program.

It should be noted that these books may have what appear to be errors compared to more recent research. These authors did not have access to many of the current online research sources that are available today. Their work should be judged on the basis of what was available to them at the time of their publications.

Both of these efforts are very important in their own ways, and still offer superb insights into the series.

Suspense *Logs*

There have been other *Suspense* logs produced over the years, especially by collector, OTR newsletter publisher (*Hello Again*), and Friends of Old Time Radio convention host Jay Hickerson.

Jerry Haendiges has researched many logs for many series and posted them online in the late 1990s. His *Suspense* log can be found at his site http://otrsite.com/logs/logs1003.htm

… and the RadioGoldindex listings, which also include plotlines for many of the episodes, is at http://www.radiogoldindex.com/cgi-local/p2.cgi?ProgramName=Suspense

The Challenge of Finding Missing Shows and Versions

As the hobby has matured, and as groups like OTRR and reputable commercial dealers release well-researched sets, many of the older *Suspense* collections are pushed out of circulation. For those interested in just listening to the programs and not any more complex collecting specialty, this is great. It's a great benefit of collecting programs today.

Some of us veteran collectors have developed specific interests in particular series or other historical aspects of the radio era. In this regard, the inadvertent elbowing out of circulation of older collections makes collecting more difficult. Some rare versions of programs in older or lesser quality sets just disappear! This means that any time a collection of reels from the 1970s or an early digitized set from the 1990s comes around, the interest of some of us veteran collectors is piqued. We are still finding versions of programs and unique recordings in mp3 sets from the late 1990s, even those at low encode rates.

Now we know that dismissing the old reel collections of long-time or deceased collectors as irrelevant is a mistake.

But there's also another prevalent belief among newer collectors: all of the programs that ever circulated in the hobby can be found in digital format today.

That is a mistaken assumption.

Old collections, analog or digital, can still have worthwhile recordings. As mentioned earlier, a missing version of *Donovan's Brain* was found by a collector searching through commercial cassettes he had purchased in the late 1970s. That version had fallen out of circulation among collectors and was forgotten.

Some of the *Roma Wines* two-per-week period (December 1943 to September 1944) broadcast recordings were found in some of these older collections.

In 2018, I found some east and west coast recordings that had fallen out of circulation in a reel collection of a deceased collector who was active in the hobby in the early 1970s. It also seemed he had access to a few of the production tapes of *Suspense* after the move away from transcription discs. In 2019 some older collectors who traded in the 1970s contacted me about transferring their reels to digital formats. What a surprise it was to find close-to-disc recordings of programs that had been circulating in bad sound for decades! Some of their other recordings of other programs were close to original sources, even for some home recordings. This meant that these recordings had not been subject to the efforts of collectors through the years to make the programs sound better. We had a fresh recording, with original defects, that could be processed through modern audio software, resulting in a much improved recording.

It's worth the effort, time, and spending, to seek out older collections. There are many programs that still need to be digitized and others than can be enhanced by modern methods.

Technology Paradox: Digital Collecting May be Getting More Difficult

In the 1990s, there was great excitement about being able to put radio programs online for Internet access. The cost and time and shipping costs of collecting on reels and cassettes and even CDs were gone.

Since that time, Internet collecting of radio programs has changed greatly. The open Internet, where many collectors posted their collections in the late 1990s and early 2000s, were indexed by Google and other search engines and recordings could be found easily. That OTR-friendly Internet is disappearing. These online collections were critical to this research in its early years, but can no longer be so, which is disappointing.

There are already fewer sets of shows being posted on personal websites. In the early years of digital OTR, there were collectors who put portions of their collections online or shared them through UseNet groups. Though collectors regularly search the Internet for recordings through Google and other search engines, the decline in the number of online recordings listed in this manner is notable.

The Internet Archive (archive.org, cited often in this book) still has some of the older collections, and some unique items have been found there.

In the mid- and late 2000s, peer-to-peer computer networks were also common. OTR fans shared their collections openly and generously. Peer networks are in decline because they are considered unsafe from a computer security and privacy perspective, no longer considered to be convenient. It is thought that programs can be found in many other easier and safer ways.

Instead, collectors are using cloud storage services like Dropbox that are not indexed by search engines.

Fear Not: Recordings are Still Being Discovered

While some of the detective work of collecting is getting much harder, collectors are still finding programs and gathering more information about *Suspense*.

It is essential to keep an eye and an ear out for access to collections that might be helpful. New and veteran collectors are always finding new recordings and can discover facts and oddities just by listening to the shows and documenting them. It was a new collector who brought renewed attention to the special twice-a-week Roma Wines run... its details had been ignored by collectors for decades.

There are always quirks in recordings that make collecting

interesting, such as in the January 30, 1947 recordings of "Three Blind Mice" where there are dialogue changes after the mid-show commercial. One starts with "Does the defendant wish to make..." and the other starts with "The defendant will rise..." Why? Is this an East Coast / West Coast pair? Is one a rehearsal? There are many other interesting aspects and quirks of this series that remain to be found.

Performances of Missing Suspense Episodes in Non-US Productions

Suspense scripts were used in Australia by Grace Gibson Productions in the series *Theatre of Thrills* (1950-1951) and *Tension* (1956-1957). The *Tension* series re-used some of the previous *Theatre of Thrills* scripts. If you're not familiar with Australian radio drama, the biography "Yes, Miss Gibson" is a

fascinating look at this Australian radio pioneer (from Texas!). The book has many insights into the general history of radio drama and the nature of business and production management in that era. https://www.amazon.com/Yes-Miss-Gibson-Australian-legend/dp/1925209164

All 52 episodes of *Tension* are available and can be ordered at the Gibson site http://gracegibsonradio.com/product/tension/ . (Note: prices are in Australian dollars and purchases can be made in US dollars via PayPal).

It appears that 23 of the 52 *Tension* scripts are *Suspense* scripts and the others are from sources such as *Theater of Famous Radio Players, Hollywood Theater* (sponsored in the US by Skippy and LaRosa, and was also syndicated) and Ziv's *Your Movietown Radio Theater.* These US shows may have shared production scripts, too! A *Lights Out* and at least one *Molle Mystery Theater* episode were also part of the *Tension* series.

One of the *Tension* productions is a missing *Suspense* episode, *The Keenest Edge.* It is well done. Many *Tension* productions are also missing episodes of the aforementioned non-*Suspense* series.

At least one *Suspense* script was used on *Caltex Star Theatre. Till the Day I Die* was the second episode of the anthology series, which began in 1947, and is often compared to the US *Lux Radio Theatre.*

Grace Gibson's company also negotiated for use of US scripts in new Australian productions. In some cases, such as the US series *Night Beat*, the Australian version proved very popular and had a longer broadcast life than the US production did, adding its own original episodes after the US production ceased.

Gibson Productions staff edited US scripts to adjust for differences in US and Australian slang, grammar, terms, and geographies. The *Suspense* episode *The Leading Citizen of Pratt County* was edited to become *The Leading Citizen of Pratt <u>District</u>* for *Tension.*

Other times, titles would change to be more appropriate for subtle differences in language or local tastes. The *Suspense* episode *Murder of Necessity* would become <u>*Crime*</u> *of Necessity* in its Australian presentation. The reason for the title change is not particularly clear other than an editor believed it made more sense for its audience or felt it was just a better title.

In the United Kingdom, the BBC series *Appointment with Fear* also mirrored some *Suspense* scripts as penned by John Dickson Carr https://en.wikipedia.org/wiki/John_Dickson _Carr.

The format of the series is much like *Suspense* because Carr played a large role in the initial design of the *Suspense* series. The early episodes of *Suspense* certainly have the feel of British drama because of his involvement. Only four recordings of *Appointment with Fear* exist. Among the *Suspense* scripts that Carr used in the series were *Cabin B-13*, *The Burning Court*, *Dealings of Mr. Markham*, and *The Pit and the Pendulum*, *The Bride Vanishes*, *Till Death Do Us Part*, and *The Devil's Saint*. The missing *Suspense* episode *The Hangman Won't Wait* was produced for *Appointment with Fear* as *The Clock Strikes Eight*, and is one of the few existing recordings of this series. The network also produced a later series, *The Man in Black*. As of this writing, it seems that none of the *The Man in Black* programs have survived.

Some of this information is from "The Sound of Suspense" which appeared in the October 1978 issue of mystery fan magazine *Armchair Detective* by Francis Nevins. Appreciation is also extended to UK old time radio experts and collectors Graeme Stevenson, Tony Lang, and Roger Bickerton.

A South African *Suspense* series was produced on Springbok Radio, but our research indicates they did not use US scripts. A correspondence between Australian OTR collector and expert Ian Grieve with Springbok expert Frans Erasmus shed some light on the series. It was indicated there were two separate *Suspense* runs on Springbok Radio. The first was from 1968 to 1972, produced by Michael McCabe, with most scripts written by him.

The second *Suspense* run started in 1984 with original scripts and multiple production companies. The series *Hitchcock's Half Hour* ran from 1977 to 1983, produced by McCabe and was "exactly the same as *Suspense*, even the same signature theme was used."

McCabe was a prolific scripter and producer [*Beyond Midnight*, *SF68*, *The Avengers*, and many others], and had a career that is a worthy research topic in itself.

For some *Suspense* episodes, recordings of professional overseas productions are the only surviving performances of *Suspense* scripts for missing US programs. These non-US productions have not received much research attention. They are worthy of future study that would be a major contribution to radio research.

What are the "Best" Suspense *Episodes?*

Great! You decide you want to listen to Suspense, but you want to listen to the best episodes or ones that have an interesting plotline. How do you decide? There are many resources.

Aside from the episode summaries in Martin Grams' book about *Suspense*, now back in print, there are other online resources that are worth viewing, especially for new collectors. The websites offer illuminating background about individual episodes, performers, and their source materials.

 There are brief descriptions about *Suspense* episodes at RadioGoldindex http://radiogoldindex.com/cgi-local/p2.cgi?ProgramName=Suspense These are best described as "teaser" descriptions of episodes, but many entries have references to other performances in *Suspense* or other series, notes about flubs or production peculiarities. In recent revisions to the listings, descriptions of *Suspense* TV shows have been added.

Some sites offer critiques and reviews of individual episodes. A favorite is the site *"Escape and Suspense"* http://www.escape-suspense.com/

Christine Miller has assured me in correspondence that she does intend to keep the site up and will resume posting new reviews sometime in the future, but there are no new posts since 2014. The entries include references to the original stories if they were adapted and provides some background on the players. It's a really a nice contribution to radio research and her insights and the way she integrates outside research into her commentary raises interest in the series.

"Old Time Radio Review" adds reviews of individual episodes on a somewhat irregular basis but it is clear that the site is actively maintained.
http://www.oldtimeradioreview.com/suspense.html

"OTR Plot Spot" has 200+ *Suspense* listings with brief comments about many of the shows and some interesting references to other series and the original works
http://www.otrplotspot.com/suspense.html

The *"Awake at Midnight"* site offers brief comments for some select episodes and rates them on an A-F scale.
http://www.awakeatmidnight.com/suspense/

To see the newest reviews go to their page that lists them by entry date. This is an excellent resource for those unfamiliar with the series who desire to sample the best episodes first.
http://www.oldtimeradioreview.com/updates.html

Other Research Resources

Newspapers.com (owned by genealogy site Ancestry.com) www.newspapers.com

Other genealogical sites have newspaper archives. It's best to check the resources at your local library as they often have access to the premium services of these sites.

Old Time Radio Researchers now has an extensive library of scanned magazines http://www.otrr.org/pg06b_magazines.htm

Scripts archives – for example, William Spier papers are at the University of Wisconsin Madison at the Wisconsin Historical Society Archives; California's Thousand Oaks Library has many holdings of scripts that OTR researchers have accessed. There are many others that can be found using Google or other search engines. Many writers and performers donated their papers to educational institutions and museums as part of their estates.

American Radio History *Billboard Magazine* searchable archive http://www.americanradiohistory.com/hd2/IDX-Business/Music/Archive-Billboard-IDX/search.cgi

Many other industry magazines are available and searchable at the home page http://www.americanradiohistory.com

Google Books books.google.com has access to many editions of *Billboard*. Be sure to include "billboard" as the first word in the search criteria.

Archive.org has many editions of *Variety Magazine* available https://archive.org/search.php? query=creator%3A%22Variety%22

The Best Unfair and Superficial History of *Suspense* You'll Ever Need

Suspense was on the air a long time. The series went through many discernible and different periods that reflected the social and economic changes from the Great Depression, the post-WW2 boom, the Cold War 1950s, and the start of JFK's "Camelot." The technology changed from radio in homes to cars and living room hi-fi systems, and from transcriptions to recording tape, and, of course, the emergence of television as a necessity. The vision behind the program changed as the entertainment business grew and the network executives, producers, directors, advertisers, and the tastes and preferences of the radio audience changed, too.

The following overly simple history of the program, provided especially for new collectors who can be more alert to how all the pieces of the series fit together, but so could some of our veteran collectors. I know I never understood the series in this way until recently. Here goes...

* * * *

Suspense began in Summer of 1942, designed to be a more thoughtful and high quality mystery program. The show was well-received but was not a major hit. The show was renewed and continued a British-style approach to mysteries. The show moved to Hollywood under the direction of William Spier to attract its performing stars to the microphone. Stories changed to be mainly faster-moving people-in-trouble productions that captured the attention of listeners, which made its ratings and reputation grow. Yet, the show had no sponsor. The performance of *Sorry, Wrong Number* started to build word-of-mouth and the attention of potential advertisers. Roma Wines started its sponsorship in December 1943.

Roma discontinued its sponsorship at the end of 1947, and the show was canceled, but some CBS executives fought to keep it on the air. They thought an hour-long format could work as it did with *Lux Radio Theatre* and also fill open air time on Saturday evenings.

It was a disaster, but CBS head William Paley was already negotiating behind the scenes with Auto-Lite for a return to the half-hour format. Paley even convinced Auto-Lite to increase the budgets and agree to sponsor a television version of the series, successful in its own way.

It was triumphant return to the half-hour format that 1948 Summer under Tony Leader, followed the next year by a return of Spier for one season. Elliott Lewis would take over the production, and when Auto-Lite left in mid-1954, leadership was given to Norman Macdonnell, followed by Antony Ellis. These were all highly talented radio professionals.

Radio legend Bill Robson led the series at a time when budgets were cut and more than half of the *Suspense* broadcasts were new (and very good) productions of prior scripts. The big Hollywood stars were gone, but marvelous and highly skilled radio veterans took their place. Fans came to enjoy Robson's introductory comments for each episode. Robson's assignment ended in August 1959. *Suspense* had top-notch production talent throughout its Hollywood era, excepting the chaos of the hour-long programs.

The show returned to its birthplace or New York City until its final cancellation in September 1962. There were some fine performances mixed with some pedestrian others, a shadow of its former greatness.

The Eras of *Suspense*			
	Start	**End**	**Producer(s)**
Forecast pilot	July 22, 1940		"Alfred Hitchcock," (Charles Vanda)
Summer series	June 17, 1942	September 30, 1942	Charles Vanda, William Spier
New York, sustained	October 27, 1942	January 19, 1943	William Spier
Hollywood, sustained	February 2, 1943	November 23, 1943	William Spier
Roma Wines 2x per week	December 2, 1943	September 21, 1944	William Spier
Roma Wines 1x per week	September 28, 1944	November 20, 1947	William Spier
Sustained	November 28, 1947	December 26, 1947	William Spier
Hour long format	January 3, 1948	May 15, 1948	William Spier, "Robert Montgomery," Anton M. Leader
Auto-Lite	July 8, 1948	June 30, 1949	Anton M. Leader
	September 1, 1949	June 29, 1950	William Spier
	August 31, 1950	June 7, 1954	Elliott Lewis
Sustained	June 15, 1954	July 20, 1954	Elliott Lewis
	July 27, 1954	December 16, 1954	Norman Macdonnell
	December 23, 1954	October 16, 1956	Antony Ellis
Robson, recording tape productions, sustained	October 23, 1956	August 23, 1959	William N. Robson
Return to New York	August 30, 1959	November 27, 1960	Paul Roberts
	June 25, 1961	May 27, 1962	Bruno Zirato, Jr.
	June 3, 1962	September 30, 1962	Fred Hendrickson

NOTE: names in quotes refers to person as producer or director "in name only" for publicity; (parentheses) refers to the likely executive in charge; list does not include "relief" producers who covered for vacations or other absences; there were NYC productions in 1947 and 1953 but these were under Hollywood management and direction.

The Missing Shows

The following is an analysis of the missing shows as of the date of this document. Many of the missing episodes were also re-performed on other dates. While certain performances of those scripts are missing, we at least have those repeat performances to fall back on.

The ones that are most sought after are one-time performances, identified in this listings *__in bold italics with double underscore__*. There are thirteen single-performance shows missing, three in 1942 and two in 1951, and the other eight scattered through the years. If you have a show that is on this list, please be sure to check the other performances noted for some shows in case it is a mislabeled show.

Some plotlines in this list are from Martin Grams' book. Others are from newspaper clippings with show details. Since the previous edition, however, we have had generous benefactors who have shared copies of the scripts of the missing programs. This has allowed us to provide more details about the programs than was possible before.

Please note that the early weeks of *Suspense* are poorly documented, and that is detailed in a separate chapter. Newspaper listings in these weeks are highly unreliable, and some of the dates of newspaper clips do not match the dates in show logs. One gets the impression that plans for performance of particular scripts were constantly changing until the series hit a firm production stride in the Fall of 1942. The clipping from the *Mason City Globe-Gazette* shows that many episodes were in development but the order of performances, even at that late date, had not been finalized.

From the June 13, 1942
Mason City Iowa Globe-Gazette

Famous Actors to Star in New Mystery Dramas

Celebrated actors of Broadway and Hollywood star in a new series of mystery adventures, entitled "Suspense," which starts over KGLO-CBS Wednesday.

The best work of distinguished detective novelists is to be dramatized during the "Suspense" series each Wednesday from 9:30 to 10 p. m.

Some of the thrillers to be heard are:

"The Burning Court," by John Dickson Carr.

"Suspicion," by Dorothy Sayers.

"The Lodger," by Mrs. Belloc Lowndes.

"Night Must Fall," by Emlyn Williams.

Charles Vanda produces and directs. The radio adaptations are done by Hal Medford, veteran radio writer who has obtained leave of absence from M-G-M studios to do the job.

Which of the hair-raising tales is to be done first has not yet been decided, but will be announced soon by Vanda.

Suspense did not get much coverage in the newspapers when it went on the air, except for the initial announcement of the series.

● *1942-07-01 The Life of Nellie James* -- **Jeanne Cagney** (**only performance on** *Suspense*); the script notes the cast originally included Loretta Young, but she was replaced.

```
ANNC'R:      The Columbia Network takes pleasure in presenting Miss
             Jeanne Cagney
             Loretta Young -- as this week's star of --

             (HARP GLISS BUILDING TO OPENING THEME...THROUGH;)

             "SUSPENSE":
```

The June 24, 1942 *Chicago Tribune* has this description: *"The hatchet murders of Nellie James' family provide the thrill on Columbia's new Suspense mystery series... 'The Life of Nellie James,' an original radio play by Harold Medford is the title of the script."*

The story is similar to the real-life murders in Fall River, Massachusetts in the late 1800s for which Lizzie Borden was tried and acquitted. In this case, the events are in Missouri, and the conclusion is also unclear as to whether Nellie actually committed the crime, just as it was for Lizzie Borden.

● *1942-07-08 Rope* -- **Richard Widmark** (**only performance on** *Suspense*) is based on the 1929 play inspired by the Leopold & Loeb murder case of 1924. https://en.wikipedia.org/wiki/Rope_%28play%29

 The play became a 1948 movie by Alfred Hitchcock https://en.wikipedia.org/wiki/Leopold_a nd_Loeb.

The July 1, 1942 *Mason City Iowa Globe-Gazette* describes it as: *A murder mystery, 'Rope,' by Patrick Hamilton, is dramatized on ... 'Suspense' series... Charles Vanda directs this story about an adventurous murderer and his weak-minded accomplice.*

ANNCR: Tonight, the play ("Rope") the thrilling London stage
           success by the author of the current Broadway hit,
           "Angel Street" -- Patrick Hamilton...... We ask that
           you relax -- ~~██████████████████~~ -- and watch
           what occurs in a single room of a well-appointed big-city
           apartment....during a period of precisely twenty-eight
           minutes...(OVERTURE IN) As you see, that room is quite
           dark -- as we raise the curtain on - "Rope"!

Suspense is using the popularity of Patrick Hamilton's *Angel Street*, playing on Broadway at the time, and the lingering success of *Rope* in London and Broadway, even though they were many years ago. On Broadway, its title was *Rope's End* because there was a different Broadway play a couple of years earlier that used the name *Rope*.

- *1942-07-15 Witness on the Westbound Train* -- **unknown cast (only performance on *Suspense*)** is based on the 1937 movie of a similar name. The description and cast of the movie is at the Internet Movie Data Base http://www.imdb.com/title/tt0029755/?ref_=nv_sr_1

The plotline is a man survives a train wreck, and later meets up with the saboteur who caused the wreck. He has to stop the saboteur from striking again.

ANNC'R: This is the account of a train trip - a tale of anxious travelers in a fabulous ride through the night .. There was young Mark Melton, for instance - the Pacific Coast detective in Lower Ten. There was Death, the restless passenger who couldn't sleep .. (DISTANT, MOURNFUL WAIL OF A TRAIN WHISTLE) And there was the witness .. (OVERTURE IN) - "The Witness On The West-Bound Train!

The script notes the date as 1942-07-15 with the title *The Witness on the West-Bound Train*. There are some logs that list this as 1942-07-22, but that is being proven to be incorrect. Some logs have the title as *Witness on the West-Bound Limited*, which is the title of the movie.

- **1942-07-22 Finishing School** -- Margo (also performed on 1943-12-30, with that performance sponsored by Roma Wines). The July 22, 1942 *Wisconsin State Journal* notes it as a "story of events at a girls' school."
The story is based on the novel *The Third Eye* by Ethel Lina White. She was the author of the famous novel *The Lady Vanishes* which became an early Alfred Hitchcock film, and a successful one, at that. This program's title, *Finishing School*, was assigned by the *Suspense* producers. For many years, because newspaper listings implied such, it was believed that *The Third Eye* was the name of a separate broadcast. See the chapter of this book about the summer 1942 season of *Suspense* for more details.

- **1942-07-29 Philomel Cottage** -- Alice Frost (also performed on 1943-10-07 with Orson Welles and again on 1946-12-26 with Lily Palmer, sponsored by Roma Wines). The program is adapted from a 1924 Agatha Christie short story, *Love from a Stranger*, which was adapted into a play in 1936. This is the first episode that William Spier was assigned as producer.

- **1942-08-12 Suspicion** -- Pedro De Cordoba (also performed on 1944-02-10 with Charles Ruggles and an hour-long version 4/3/48 with Alan Reed).

- **1943-01-26 Death Went Along for the Ride** -- Ralph Bellamy (also performed on 1944-04-27 with Gene Kelly)

- *1943-02-09 The Hangman Won't Wait* -- Sydney Greenstreet (part 1 exists, which means that the second transcription disc with the last 15 minutes is lost or damaged; need full episode) (only performance on *Suspense*)

The complete show has been recreated by American Radio Theater and the recording is at http://amerad.libsyn.com/suspense-hangman-wontwait

The script is by John Dickson Carr and is included in an anthology of Carr writings *The Door to Doom and Other Detections*.

It was also adapted for the BBC's *Appointment with Fear* as "The Clock Strikes Eight," a recording of which is in circulation. https://archive.org/details/AppointmentWithFear440518TheClockStrikesEight

- *1943-02-23 Will You Walk into My Parlor?* -- Geraldine Fitzgerald (only part 1 exists; need full episode) (only performance on *Suspense*)
  - According to the article *The Sound of Suspense*, written by Francis Nevins and appearing in the October 1978 issue of *Armchair Detective*, the script was printed in the September 1945 edition of *Ellery Queen Mystery Magazine*.

The February 23, 1943 *Mason City IA Globe Gazette* described it as follows:

"Geraldine Fitzgerald, gifted screen star, has the principal role in 'Will You Walk Into My Parlor?' an original drama by John Dickson Carr… With this play, 'Suspense' returns to New York after several weeks in Hollywood. The story concerns a young woman, suspected by her fiance of having poisoned three husbands. Author Carr, celebrated mystery story writer, has built it up to a surprising climax."

The complete show has been recreated by American Radio Theater and the recording is at <u>amerad.libsyn.com/</u> <u>suspense-step-into-my-parlor</u>

- **1943-03-02 The Night Reveals** -- Fredric March (also performed on 1943-12-09 with Robert Young, 1946-04-18 with Keenan Wynn, and 1949-05-26 with Fredric March sponsored by Auto-Lite)

- ***1943-03-09 The Phantom Archer* -- Ralph Bellamy (only performance on *Suspense*)**; the radio script was by John Dickson Carr. The script can be found in an anthology of Carr writings *The Door to Doom and Other Detections* and was also in the June 1948 edition of *Ellery Queen Mystery Magazine* according to the Nevins article previously cited. Nevins describes the story as *"On an island off the Cornish coast, a woman is killed by an arrow fired from the end of a long portrait gallery which is inhabited only by a wooden dummy in an archer's costume."*

In addition to Bellamy, the case included Walter Hampden (known for his Broadway roles and a role in *The Hunchback of Notre Dame*), Muriel Kirkland (also known for her Broadway roles and was the wife of famed radio actor Staats Cotsworth), and Constance Collier (Broadway actress, appeared in silent films, acting teacher known for helping silent film actors adapt to the sound era of motion pictures). Collier also appeared in Hitchcock's adaptation of *Rope*.

```
NARRATOR:      Such a mysterious, unusual crime.  Such an extraordinary
               way to commit a murder.  In London homes everywhere
               people were reading about it from the newspapers.

WOMAN'S        'St. Iyes, Cornwall,  July 15th, 1938'.
VOICE:

MAN'S          'Harriet, Lady Drew---elderly widow of the late
VOICE:         Sir George Drew -- was mysteriously slain tonight at
               .St. Ives Castle , on an island off the Cornish coast.'

SECOND         'The means of death is said to have been an arrow---'
MAN'S VOICE:
```

The episode is about a series of mysterious killings in a 1938 London castle by being struck by an arrow, with no suspects for the crimes. The wooden archer mentioned above has no mechanism inside to shoot arrows. Suspicion moves to the people already in the house. And there's a parrot in the story to scream whenever something is about to happen.

- **1943-03-16 Cabin B-13** -- Ralph Bellamy (also performed on 1943-11-09 with Margo and Philip Dorn); the University of Wisconsin script archive shows the title as "Cabin B-Thirteen." This John Dickson Carr episode would lead to a brief CBS radio mystery series of the same name.

 It would and also become the basis of the movie *Dangerous Crossing* http://www.imdb.com/title/tt0045669/

The movie can often be found on YouTube or other online services.

 A trailer for *Dangerous Crossing* can be viewed at https://archive.org/details/DangerousCrossingTrailer

- _**1945-07-26 Fury and Sound**_ -- **Norman Lloyd** (only performance on *Suspense*).

The Darryl Shelton book about *Suspense* includes the short story adaptation that originally appeared in Suspense Magazine #1 .

An upcoming chapter of this book discusses the four-issue run of *Suspense Magazine*.

An AFRS transcription sold on eBay on 2013-12-06 for $405.

The July 26, 1945 *Decatur IL Daily Review* description is: *"Norman Lloyd and Mark Humbolt co-star in 'Fury and Sound,' a drama concerning a thwarted assistant producer driven by the violent ego of his employer to murder."*

 *Blue Hours Productions* recorded a performance in 2015 that became available in 2017; performances are at https://soundcloud.com/suspenseradiodrama

The script was performed on the syndicated Ziv TV series, *The Unexpected* and starred Hans Conried. http://www.imdb.com/title/tt0736763/

The TV performance of *Fury and Sound* is available on the DVD "Obscure Horror TV" at classicmoviesdvd.com (many thanks to author Martin Grams for information about the TV presentation)

This is one of the most interesting episodes in the entire *Suspense* series, so interesting that there is a chapter of this book devoted specifically to it. Was co-star Mark Humbolt a real person? *No!* There's more shenanigans behind the scenes, too.

- *1946-02-28 The Keenest Edge* -- **Richard Greene (only performance on Suspense)**; the script for this show is in the Darryl Shelton book. Greene success was mainly in Great Britain, and he became most popular in the *Robin Hood* television series that ran in the late 1950s.

```
                          SUSPENSE

                   PRESENTED BY ROMA WINES

                      "THE KEENEST EDGE"

                         STARRING

                    MR. RICHARD GREENE
                                          5:00 - 5:30 PM PST
     THURSDAY, FEBRUARY 28, 1946          9:00 - 9:30 PM PST

   BRADLEY:   Now....Roma Wines....R-O-M-A....Made in California

              for enjoyment throughout the world....Roma Wines

              present....(KNIFE CHORD)

   NARR:      SUSPENSE!

   MUSIC:     (KNIFE CHORD....HOLD UNDER)

   NARR:      Tonight Roma Wines bring you Mr. Richard Greene as

              star of "The Keenest Edge"...A suspense Play...produced,

              edited, and directed for Roma Wines by William Spier.
```

The show was produced in Australia by Grace Gibson Productions in their series *Tension*. A recording is included in their 2016 collection of the series http://gracegibsonradio.com/product/tension/ , and its production is well done.

A recreation of the show was performed by American Radio Theater http://amerad.libsyn.com/suspense-the-keenest-edge

- **1947-03-20 The Waxwork** -- Claude Rains (also performed on 1956-05-01 with William Conrad and 1959-03-01 with Herbert Marshall).

This episode is interesting not because of what it is, but what it could have been: Alfred Hitchcock in a radio drama. In December, 1946, *Variety* and columnist Louella Parsons stated that Hitchcock would appear on *Suspense* on December 26, 1946 in *The Waxwork*. That did not occur, but at the close of the performance of *Philomel Cottage*, Hitchcock was mentioned as an upcoming guest star of *Suspense* in the coming weeks (at the end of the East Coast broadcast, Hitchcock's name was actually flubbed as "Alexander Hitchcock"!). Hitchcock never appeared on *Suspense*.

```
                        "SUSPENSE"

                  PRESENTED BY ROMA   INES

                     "THE WAXWORK"
        (REVISED)
                        STARRING

                   MR. CLAUDE RAINS
                              5:00  -  5:30  PM PST
  THURSDAY, MARCH 20, 1947           9:00  -  9:30  PM PST


  BRADLEY:    Yes, ROMA wines taste better ... because only   ROMA

              selects from the world's greatest wine reserves .. for

              your pleasure!

              (PAUSE)

              And now .. Roma Wines... R-O-M-A ... ROMA Wines present.

  MUSIC:      KNIFE CHORD

  NARR:       "SUSPENSE"

  MUSIC:      (KNIFE CHORD ... HOLD UNDER)

  NARR:       Tonight, ROMA Wines bring you Mr. Claude Rains in "The

              Waxwork" ... a SUSPENSE play ... produced, edited and

              directed for ROMA Wines by William Spier.
```

- **1947-03-27 Trial by Jury** -- Nancy Kelly, sponsored by Roma Wines (also performed on 1957-06-16 with Nancy Kelly and William N. Robson as producer).

- **1947-07-17 Beyond Good and Evil** -- Vincent Price (previously performed on 1945-10-11 with Joseph Cotten); *this program may exist as an aircheck, still being investigated.*

  The July 17, 1947 *Decatur IL Herald* described it as: *"Vincent Price stars as an escaped convict who assumes the identity of a minister when Suspense presents an encore performance of the Ben Hecht-Douglas Whitney story..."*

- **1947-12-19 Wet Saturday** -- Boris Karloff (previously performed on 1942-06-24 with Clarence Derwent, 1943-12-16 with Charles Laughton, and later performed on 1948-03-20 with Dennis Hoey as half of an hour-long program)

- **1948-01-31 Bet with Death** -- Lee Bowman in an hour-long format (also performed on 1942-11-10 as "Will You Make a Bet with Death?"). The January 31, 1948 *Bakersfield Californian* described it as: *"Robert Montgomery is an old hand at the grim business of carrying a friend's head around in a basket and this week's offering, 'Bet with Death' is in the Montgomery tradition of diabolical mayhem and murder."*

- **_1948-07-08 The Last Chance_ -- Cary Grant (only performance on *Suspense*);.** This is the first Auto-Lite episode, returning to the half-hour format after the disappointing hour-long run. The change to Auto-Lite brought new life to the series, making this episode of great importance in the history of *Suspense*.

The July 8, 1948 *Mason City IA Globe-Gazette* described it as: *"Cary Grant stars in the gripping melodrama 'The Last Chance'… Auto-Lite's new series of psychological chillers will star the most high-powered line-up of big name film stars to be found anywhere on the airwaves this summer."*

The *Variety* review of this episode (on an upcoming page) lists the author as Larry Marcus, but the front of the script identifies it as a Les Crutchfield adaptation of a Lou Lusty short story, and that was used in publicity. But the last page lists Larry Marcus. It's probably Crutchfield.

THE SHREVEPORT TIMES, SUNDAY, JULY 4, 1948

'SUSPENSE' RETURNS TO AIR ON CBS-KWKH

Gary Grant to Star in Premiere Story, "The Last Chance;" Other Top Stars Follow

"Suspense," the award-winning psychological drama series, returns to the air Thursday at 8 p.m. over CBS-KWKH. Cary Grant, who launched "Suspense" on its first commercial series in 1943 will star in the premiere broadcast of this new series. His vehicle is "The Last Chance" the story of a man given only one week to live. It is based on a story by Lou Lusty and adapted to radio by Les Crutchfield.

Tonight's Suspense play was written by Larry Marcus. The music was composed by Lucien Moraweck and conducted by Lud Gluskin. The entire production was under the direction of Anton M. Leader. Next Thursday, same time, you will hear Ida Lupino in "SUMMER NIGHT".

Variety reviewed the first Auto-Lite episode in its 1948-07-14 edition.

SUSPENSE
("The Last Chance")
With Cary Grant, Paul Frees, Sheppard Menkin, Hermand Waldman, Maxine Marx, Fred Campbell, John T. Smith, Daws Butler, Berry Kroeger, Stanley Farrar; Lud Gluskin, conductor; Lucien Moroweck, arranger; Frank Martin, announcer
Writer: Larry Marcus
Producer-Director: Anton Leader
30 Mins.; Thurs., 9 p.m.
AUTO-LITE
CBS, from Hollywood
(*Newell-Emmett*)

The Auto-Lite sponsorship of "Suspense" merges an advertiser and a program that had bumpy careers last season. The ignition supply firm had its troubles bankrolling a Dick Haymes show against the Al Jolson-Kraft stanza and the rest of the Thursday night lineup on NBC. And "Suspense" had its misadventures in shifting to full-hour format, becoming a regular vehicle for Robert Montgomery and having its original producer, William Spier, succeeded by Anton Leader.

The present setup promises 'a somewhat better situation for everyone concerned. The show itself is back to half-hour length, which seems best for a trick-formula series of this sort. It has a policy of using various stars, thereby permitting greater story flexibility than possible when every script must suit the same star (although a single star in the same, continuing characterization may tend to build a following). Finally, in Leader it has a producer-director of demonstrated ability. As for Auto-Lite, it seemingly has better prospects of bucking the comedy-variety competition on NBC with a dramatic thriller series than with a musical program. Finally, this is another CBS sale of its own production to a client.

The premiere of the series, last Thursday night (8), offered Cary Grant in Larry Marcus' adaptation of a Lou Lusty skin-tingler titled "The Last Chance." A yarn about a crooked gambler tracked down by the unseen, relentless brother of one of his victims, the piece was a first-person narrative-into-flashbacks, with a phone conversation to set the climax and terse, eloquent sound effects for the grisly payoff. It was artfully scripted (with only a couple of tiny holes), skillfully produced and persuasively played. Grant was excellent in the long part of the harried prey, while Stanley Farrar, Sheppard Menkin and Fred Campbell were effective in supporting parts.

The Auto-Lite commercial pattern was unusual for a dramatic show. There was an opening plug in the form of a dramatized commercial (father, mother and son at a service station and listening to the broadcast on their car radio), a sponsor-identification cut-in at approximately 10 minutes, and another major dramatized plug at the close, with a sign-off jingle. It was good integration of commercial and program, though the dramatized idea may quickly wear out, if continued. *Hobe.*

● *1950-06-15 Deadline* -- **Broderick Crawford** (only performance on *Suspense*); The script is by John Monsos. The June 15, 1950 *Marysville OH Tribune* described the show as: "Broderick Crawford, Oscar aside, will get tough in the leading role of *'Deadline'*..." The June 15, 1950 *Atlanta Constitution* says that Crawford is "appearing as an ambitious newspaper editor who is too much of an eager beaver whit it comes to scooping rival papers in matters of crime, Crawford skyrockets the circulation of his paper... until he makes the mistake of publishing the story of a killing an hour before it takes place."

The cast include Joe Kearns, Jay Novello, Georgia Ellis, John Hoyt, and Tony Barrett. Spier produced, Norman Macdonnell directed, Lud Gluskin directed the music, and Harlow Wilcox was the announcer.

The drama portion was recorded on June 3, 1950... on a Saturday night!

```
THURSDAY, JUNE 15, 1950


Author:    John S. Monsos
REHEARSAL:   Studio Two
Cast & Sound:
           6/3/50 - 7:00-12:00 PM
Music:              2:30-6:00
```

There is a *Radio City Playhouse* episode with the same title was written by John Bethune and is about a drama critic. That was believed to be an early production of this Monsos script, but that was incorrect.

- **1950-09-07 The Tip** -- Ida Lupino (also performed on 1954-07-06 with Lurene Tuttle). The cast included Herb Butterfield, Harry Bartell, Joe Kearns, Jerry Hausner, Hy Averback, and Henry Blair

- **1951-05-24 Fresh Air, Sunshine and Murder** -- Jeff Chandler (also performed as *Rub Down and Out* on 1958-07-06 with Lloyd Bridges) The May 24, 1951 *Tucson Daily Citizen* describes it as: *"'Fresh Air, Sunshine and Murder' stars Jeff Chandler as a guy who steals a mobster's girl and winds up at a drive-in movie."*

```
#39  Thursday, May 24, 1951                    (REVISED)



                    AUTO - LITE Presents

                         SUSPENSE

                         Starring
                     MR. JEFF CHANDLER

                            in
                 "Fresh Air, Sunshine and Murder"


                           CAST
             ZACK...............JEFF CHANDLER
             JOYCE..............CATHY LEWIS
             BIG WILLY..........LOU MERRILL
             FRANKIE............HERB VIGRAN
             BENNY..............CLAYTON POST
             OBLO...............JACK KRUSCHEN
             STU
             HENRY..............JOSEPH KEARNS



       Rehearsal:
       cast:  5/23 - 8:00 to 12:00m  Studio 1
              5/24 - 4:30 to 6:00    Studio 2
       orch:  5/24 - 3:00 to 6:00    Studio 1
       AIR:         6:00 -- 6:30
```

● **1951-11-05 Trials of Thomas Shaw -- Joseph Cotten** (also performed on 1955-11-15 as *Once a Murderer* with Ben Wright). Note that the script cover image below has the casting for *Once a Murderer* written over the original *Trials of Thomas Shaw* casting. In the plotline, a man is found innocent of murder for lack of evidence, and he decides to try to get away with it again.

● <u>*1951-11-12 Mission of the Betta*</u> -- **John Hodiak (only performance on** *Suspense*). A submarine is on a special mission to transport Australians from Japanese territory to the US prior to the start of WW2. The November 12, 1951 *Tucson Daily Citizen* described it as *"John Hodiak stars in a thrilling submarine tale, 'The Mission of the Betta'."*

The *Shreveport Times* of November 11, 1951 reported (based on CBS-supplied information) that the episode was *"Based on a heroic submarine mission in the Pacific... the tense documentary drama tells how the sub's commander... carries out an order to rescue a dozen men from a Japanese-held island, under heavy enemy fire...The submarine's deadly game of hide and seek with Japanese destroyers, and its bold attacks on enemy battleships, provide other highlights in the taut drama. Descriptions of the fighting, and maneuvering of the sub are among the most vivid and accurate ever presented on the air."*
The cast also included Ed Max, Harry Bartell, Jerry Hausner, Joe Kearns, Jack Smight, Charles Calvert, Clayton Post, and Ben Wright. Harlow Wilcox announced, and Larry Thor was the narrator.

The script is written by "Christopher Anthony" which is a pseudonym of William N. Robson. There are more details about the use of this name in a separate chapter. About three script pages of the dialogue for this episode were used in a 1943 episode of *Man Behind the Gun* which had a different plotline. That episode, *Incident in the Pacific*, was also set in a submarine. Robson was particularly proud of that series which appreciated the heroism and skills of those serving in WW2's European and Pacific fronts.

The actors were positioned in different distances in relation to the microphone to give the impression of the listener sitting in a fixed position inside the submarine.

The 1943 performance of the *Man Behind the Gun* episode *Incident in the Pacific* is not in circulation, but the repeat 1944 performance is, and can be found at www.otrrlibrary.org.

```
                                          SUSPENSE -1-
                                          11-12-51

 1  RAMSEY:    Log of the United States Submarine Betta. Thirteen
 2             September 1942. Fifteen hundred thirty hours. Outward
 3             bound from Pearl Harbor for seventh Pacific Patrol.
 4             Clearing Net and Boom defenses on the surface, making
 5             six knots.
 6  SOUND:     LAP OF WAVES AGAINST BOAT. WIND.
 7  RAMSEY:    Ten degrees right rudder. Course two two five.
 8  Q.M.       Ten degrees right air. Course is now two two five
 9  RAMSEY:    All ahead standard.
10  SOUND:     OFF BELL RINGS TWICE.
11  Q.M.:      All ahead standard she is air.
12  RAMSEY:    Rig for diving. Pass the word.
13  Q.M.:      Rig for diving. Pass the word.
14  RAMSEY:    Rig for diving. There's always a catch in your throat
15             when you give that command. For you only give it once
16             on a patrol. From now until you return to port, the
17             ship will be rigged for diving at all times. And you
18             wonder how many times you will dive, and for how many
19             reasons. And you wonder if everything aboard this
20             incredibly complicated and crowded vessel, every valve,
21             and dial, and lever, every gasket, and sea cock and
22             torpedo war head will respond to strains and stresses
23             you may have to impose upon them. And the men? No
24             you don't have to wonder about them. Six times
25             they've put to sea with you, and the eight rising sun
26             flags on your conning tower tell how they fight their
27             boat. You're sure of the men. You know how every
28             of them will react.
```

- ***1951-11-19 The Embezzler* -- John Lund (only performance on *Suspense*)**. The November 19, 1951 *Tucson Daily Citizen* describes it as: *"John Lund plays the part of a professional embezzler who finally works out a complicated plan that entangles him."*

A recreation of the show was performed by American Radio Theater http://amerad.libsyn.com/suspense-the-embezzler

```
#13   Monday, November 19, 1951              (REVISED)
(Rebroadcast locally:  9:00 - 9:30 PM)       (e) Broadcast


                   AUTO - LITE Presents

                        SUSPENSE

                        Starring

                      MR. JOHN LUND

                          in

                    "The Embezzler"

                          CAST

          DANIEL................JOHN LUND

          FRED.................LOU MERRILL

          SIMMS..............SYLVIA SIMMS

          MANAGER............STAN WAXMAN

          LETTIE.........MARY JANE CROFT

          MERRILL..............JOE KEARNS


Dir...............Lewis
Sec'y............Curcio
A.D.............McManus
Eng................Carr
Sound.............Bayz          Rehearsal:
               Murray
Comm'l........Holland           cast: 10:30 - 1:30  Studio 1
             McKennon                 3:00 - 5:00
               Simms
Anncr.........Wilcox            orch: 2:00 - 5:00
Narr...........Thor
Music.........Gluskin           AIR:  5:00 - 5:30  PM
```

- **1951-11-26 Misfortune in Pearls -- Frank Lovejoy ;** cast also included Joan Banks (Mrs. Lovejoy); AFRS copy sold on eBay on 2014-04-20 for $710. It was performed again on 1956-01-07 as *End of the String* with Stacy Harris.

A recording of *Misfortune in Pearls* may exist by a collector who had access to the disc prior to the sale; a recording has yet to appear in circulation.

The Chicago Tribune of November 25, 1951 described it as: *"Frank Lovejoy will star in 'A Misfortune in Pearls'... He will portray a dealer in cheap costume jewelry who visits a wealthy jeweler friend and becomes involved in the disappearance of a million dollar pearl necklace."*

The description in The Tucson Daily Citizen of November 26, 1951 was: *"Frank Lovejoy stars in 'A Misfortune in Pearls' and you'll have trouble deciding if he is a thief or detective."*

```
#14   Monday, November 26, 1951                      (REVISED)
(Rebroadcast locally:  9:00 - 9:30 PM)
                                        Elliot Lewis


                    AUTO - LITE Presents

                        SUSPENSE

                        Starring

                    MR. FRANK LOVEJOY

                           in

                 "A Misfortune in Pearls"

                         CAST

              MARK.............FRANK LOVEJOY

              SAM..............JOSEPH KEARNS

              COLLIE...........LARRY THOR

              JEAN.............JOAN BANKS
              MAN/
              POSTMAN..........CHARLES CALVERT

              MR. LARKIN.......SIDNEY MILLER
```

```
Dir...............Lewis
Secty.............Curcio
A.D...............McManus
Eng...............Carr            Rehearsal:
Sound.............Bays
          Murray              cast: 10:30 - 1:30   Studio 1
Comm'l............Holland             3:00 - 5:00
          Sims
Anncr.............Wilcox       orch:  2:00 - 5:00
Narr..............Thor
Music.............Gluskin      AIR:   5:00 - 5:30  PM
```

Frank Lovejoy trivia: He was the original pick to play the lead in the series *Casey, Crime Photographer.* Instead, that Summer of 1943 he went to Cape Cod with his wife, Joan Banks, to work on a play that was headed to Broadway. The play, *The Snark was a Boojum,* did open, but closed after a few nights.

- **1951-12-24 Twas the Night Before Christmas** -- Greer Garson (also performed on 1953-12-21; the 1953 show mentions the movie *Knights of the Round Table* at the open). The existing recording is often misdated.

  The description in the December 24, 1951 *Tucson Daily Citizen* was: *"There is neither hate nor murder in the plat, but this story, starring Greer Garson, is one of the most gripping plays ever broadcast..."*

- **1952-09-15 Sorry, Wrong Number** -- Agnes Moorehead (performed seven other times on the series; this one has Larry Thor as announcer and is the only Auto-Lite performance). An item from the June 5, 1952 of *The Tipton IN Daily Tribune* implies that this performance was originally scheduled for earlier in the year but canceled.

  > How come "Sorry, Wrong Number" was cancelled so abruptly in its latest "Suspense" reprise? Agnes Moorhead was scheduled for the virtuoso suffering. Too bad. It's the scariest. . . .

  Instead, the show was used to open the Fall 1952 season. This performance is notable in many ways, described in the upcoming chapter devoted to the *Sorry, Wrong Number* franchise.

- **1955-01-06 Murder Aboard the Alphabet** -- William Conrad (previously performed on 1947-08-21 with John Lund)

- **1955-08-23 Beetle and Mr. Bottle** -- Eric Snowden (also performed on 1959-09-20 with John Gibson)

- ___1956-01-03 The Eavesdropper___ -- **Lawrence Dobkin (only performance on *Suspense*)**
  A couple having an affair plans the murder of the woman's husband. After arranging their alibi, they head to the building where the murder will take place. A plumber, locked in a bathroom where he was working, overhears the murder carried out. It's a race against time to keep their alibi intact as the couple tries to kill him before he is able to call the police.

```
                          "SUSPENSE"
                           #76-5-1
                       "THE EAVESDROPPER"

AIR:  TUESDAY, JANUARY 3, 1956              5:30-5:58:50 PM

DIRECTOR:      ANTONY ELLIS        CAST       12:00 - 2:30 PM
SCRIPT SEC'Y:  SCOTTIE CUMMINGS                   and
ASSOCIATE:     KENNY McMANUS                  3:30 - 5:30 PM
ENGINEER:      BOB CHADWICK        MUSIC:     3:00 - 5:30 PM
SOUND:         BILL JAMES          ANNOUNCER: 3:30 - 5:30 PM
               TOM HANLEY          NARRATOR
MUSIC:         WILBUR HATCH        STUDIO:    C
NARRATOR:      GEORGE WALSH        AIR:       5:30 - 6:00 PM
ANNOUNCER:     ROY ROWAN
AUTHOR:        DON YERRILL

                          CAST

              DAVE.................LAWRENCE DOBKIN
              KAREN................CHARLOTTE LAWRENCE
              HARRIS...............HERB ELLIS
              BILL.................PARLEY BAER
```

- **1956-04-24 A Case of Nerves** -- Parley Baer (previously performed on 1950-06-01 with Edward G. Robinson)

- ***1956-08-01 Massacre at the Little Big Horn*** -- Stacy **Harris and John Stevenson (only performance on** *Suspense*)
The August 1, 1956 *Eugene OR Guard* described the show as: *"The story of Custer's last stand will be dramatized on* Suspense... *Entitled 'Massacre at Little Big Horn,' the broadcast will treat the tragic story with absolute historical accuracy down to the actual names of those involved. The battle of the Little Big Horn tool place on June 25, 1876."*

The cast includes Harris as the narrator, Stevenson as Custer, and Alan Reed, Larry Thor, Helen Kleeb, Ralph Moody, Don Diamond, Shepard Menken, Harry Bartell, and John W. James.

```
                        "SUSPENSE"
                        106-8-1
                "Massacre At The Little Big Horn"

                                     TC:   5:30 - 5:58:50 PM
AIR: WEDNESDAY, AUGUST 1, 1956       KNX:  8:30 - 9:00 PM

PRODUCER-DIRECTOR:  ANTONY ELLIS     CAST & CREW:  12:00-2:30;
                                                   3:30-5:30 PM
SCRIPT SECRETARY:   CHARLENE WILKERSON

ASSOCIATE:          KEN MCMANUS       MUSIC:        3:00-5:30 PM

ENGINEER:           JAMES MURPHY      ANNOUNCER:    3:30-5:30 PM

SOUND:              TOM HANLEY        AIR:          5:30-5:58:50 PM
                    BILL JAMES

MUSIC:              WILBUR HATCH       STUDIO:      C

ANNOUNCER:          ROY ROWAN

NARRATOR NO. 1:     GEORGE WALSH

AUTHOR:             CHARLES B. SMITH
```

A Concluding Word about the Missing Episodes

As of the time of this writing, there are 14 missing single-performance programs and 20 missing programs that were performed additional times. These counts do not include some of the missing east or west coast performances from the period of December 1943 to September 1944 when *Suspense* had performances on different days (Thursday and Monday) for the respective coasts.

The count does not include the period where there were two same-day performances (see the chapter about East-West performances).

The missing 14 single performances are about 1.5% of all *Suspense* scripts (including repeats), which is a stunning accomplishment for a series that lasted for so long with so many changes in production staff and technology, and performance venue.

Summary Tables of Missing Programs: Unique and Multiple Performances

Unique performances: 14 missing episodes with only one performance

DATE	TITLE
1942-07-01	Life of Nellie James
1942-07-08	Rope
1942-07-15	Westbound Limited
1943-02-09	The Hangman Won't Wait (first half of show exists)
1943-02-23	Will You Walk into My Parlor? (first half of show exists)
1943-03-09	The Phantom Archer
1945-07-26	Fury and Sound (AFRS transcription sold on eBay)
1946-02-28	The Keenest Edge
1948-07-08	The Last Chance
1950-06-15	Deadline
1951-11-12	Mission of the Betta
1951-11-19	The Embezzler
1956-01-03	The Eavesdropper
1956-08-01	Massacre at the Little Big Horn

Multiple performances:
20 missing episodes performed at other times

DATE	TITLE	OTHER PERFORMANCES
1942-07-29	Philomel Cottage	1943-10-07 and 1946-12-26
1942-08-05	Finishing School	1943-12-30
1942-08-12	Suspicion	1944-02-10 and 1948-04-03
1943-01-26	Death Went Along for the Ride	1944-04-27
1943-03-02	The Night Reveals	1943-12-09, 1946-04-18, and 1949-05-26
1943-03-16	Cabin B-13	1943-11-09
1947-03-20	The Waxwork	1956-05-01 and 1959-03-01
1947-03-27	Trial by Jury	1957-06-16
1947-07-17	Beyond Good and Evil	1945-10-11
1947-12-19	Wet Saturday	1942-06-24, 1943-12-16, and 1948-03-20
1948-01-31	Bet with Death	1942-11-10
1950-09-07	The Tip	1954-07-06
1951-05-24	Fresh Air, Sunshine and Murder	1958-07-05 as *Rub Down and Out*
1951-11-05	Trials of Thomas Shaw	1955-11-15 as *Once a Murderer*
1951-11-26	Misfortune in Pearls	1956-01-07 as *End of the String*
1951-12-24	Twas the Night Before Christmas	1953-12-21
1952-09-15	Sorry, Wrong Number	1943-05-25, 1943-08-21, 1944-02-24, 1945-09-06, 1948-11-18, 1957-10-20, and 1960-02-14
1955-01-06	Murder Aboard the Alphabet	1947-08-21
1955-08-23	Beetle and Mr. Bottle	1959-09-20
1956-04-24	A Case of Nerves	1950-06-01

Other missing or incomplete programs

The only circulating copy of the 1951-03-15 show, *Strange for a Killer*, is the recording of the dialogue portion only. A complete broadcast version is still needed. Based information documented by researcher Stewart Wright, at this time CBS was recording drama portions of many of its shows separately and then adding orchestral and announcer segments later. Therefore, this is not likely a rehearsal as often noted, but the unedited drama portion that would later be integrated with sound effects and musical bridges in the final recording made for scheduled broadcast. This script was used again in 1955 and 1959, so a full performances can be heard with those recordings.

The 1948-04-24 hour-long episode of *The Search* starring Howard Culver is missing its first 15 minutes, meaning that the first of four transcription discs or a side of a pair of transcription discs for the program was missing or damaged. It is unlikely that a replacement network copy will be found. The opening of this episode is now described in a separate chapter that allows listeners to enjoy the production in its full context.

A partial network version of 1951-04-19-51 *The Rescue* with Jimmy Stewart is missing its final 10 minutes. The audio quality of the program implies that it is a home disc recording. Luckily, a complete AFRS version of the program (#365) surfaced a few years ago.

The Early Roma Wines Shows: A New Wrinkle for OTR Collectors

When Roma Wines initiated its sponsorship of *Suspense* in December 1943, the show was aired on two different nights. The two performance schedule was announced at the end of *Suspense* broadcasts earlier in November, when it was a sustained sponsorless program. The CBS network, in the East and Central time zones, had a broadcast on Thursdays. The CBS Pacific Network had a second, new performance of that script on Mondays that was heard in the Mountain and Pacific time zones. (It is possible some Mountain cities had a choice of broadcast feeds).This lasted until mid-September 1944 when the show became a Thursday night fixture nationally. Existing recordings have been identified and have been properly dated. Details are posted at www.archive.org/details/SuspenseRoma43 to44

The day of the next broadcast is announced at the end of each program, usually as "Join us next Thursday" (which is heard on east coast programs) or "next Monday" (west coast) or a similar wording.

The list of the programs found and missing are in the table below. Also included are the AFRS versions of the shows where available. Not all of the AFRS recordings can be assigned as "East Coast" or "West Coast." AFRS would edit out the announcements that mentioned the day of the next broadcast. The exception to this would be a significant change in cast, especially the announcer, or a difference in the dramatic timing or the performance of the actors. These need to be investigated through careful listening and documentation. AFRS discs have the dates of the original programs etched around the label "in the matrix." Only those collectors who have access to AFRS transcriptions can see that information because it is hard to capture it with disc label photographs. If any collectors have access to AFRS discs from this era, they can help identify which performance AFRS used. *(Hat tip to disc collector Randy Riddle for reminding us of this)*. The upcoming chart of shows from this era includes the weekday of AFRS recording source where known.

The episode *Fugue in C Minor* that is announced as a Thursday East Coast program has some minor "flubs" which has caused the recording to be labeled as a rehearsal for many years. It is virtually certain that it is the actual Thursday broadcast. The other performance of the script for the West Coast is error-free. *Fugue* is the only episode where there are obvious dialogue differences in the two recordings. *Suspense* was usually produced error-free, especially after the famous flub at the end of the first broadcast of *Sorry, Wrong Number*, so it is easy to understand why collectors might consider any recording with a problem as a rehearsal.

There are some recordings where no day is mentioned in one broadcast but is mentioned in the other recording. For example, there is a recording that has "join us next Monday" and another recording with "join us next week." In this case, the date assigned to a recording is by simple process of elimination. There were often some changes to the supporting cast.

For example, the Thursday 1944-07-06 *Search for Henri LeFevre* has Joseph Kearns as the "Man in Black," while the Monday 1944-07-10 does not (it's John McIntire). The Thursday 1944-07-13 *Beast Must Die* does not have Kearns (it's McIntire again), but the Monday 1944-07-17 does. It seems Kearns was on a weeklong summer vacation while the 1944-07-10 and 1944-07-13 programs were broadcast. (Kearns may be more familiar to those who grew up in the 1950s and 1960s as "Mr. Wilson" on the *Dennis the Menace* TV program).

A word of thanks is owed to members of the "Cobalt Club" OTR online forum who identified many of the shows and scoured many collections to find many of the obscure recordings of this brief but interesting era of *Suspense*.

There are still many missing ones. Some were found in older encoded sets prior to the release of the first OTRR certified sets. Some of the missing recordings might exist in some old reel or cassette collections. And of course, transcriptions of the recordings are always sought.

A public spreadsheet that details the found and missing recordings is being maintained at https://docs.zoho.com/sheet/published.do? rid=uhq05acdd864923f1410ebe2894c4790beaef

Outside of this special Roma Wines period, there are other east/west recordings in the series broadcast on the same date. It was common to have live performances for the Eastern time zone and another live one for the Pacific time zone during some periods of the *Suspense* series and other series. A handful of these pairs exist, though it is possible that not all of the second performances for the Pacific network were recorded and archived. Individual performances for the coastal time zones ended in sometime in the late 1940s, especially as the use of recording tape became more common after WW2. The direction and acting performances of these pairs are usually indistinguishable in simultaneous playing for comparison; that's how well-produced Suspense usually was. The differences are minuscule.

This is what makes it difficult to determine which performance was used by AFRS when the transcription discs are not available. The AFRS discs had etchings around the disc label that usually indicated the date of the original broadcast. Of the discs that have been documented, it appears that the Thursday recordings were the ones most often used.

The check marks in the tables indicate that the recording exists in collector circulation. There are six episodes for which all three versions (East, West, AFRS) are known to exist, with four of those episodes in general circulation.

This period in the early Roma Wines sponsorship was indeed a unique situation that deserves further research, and further efforts to find and recover the missing recordings.

EAST COAST DATE	EPISODE TITLE	EAST (Thurs)	WEST (Mon, 4 days later)	AFRS (source broadcast in paren.)
1943-12-02	The Black Curtain	✓ likely **East**; says "next week"		
1943-12-09	The Night Reveals	✓		
1943-12-16	Wet Saturday	✓		✓
1943-12-23	Back for Christmas	✓		
1943-12-30	Finishing School	✓		
1944-01-06	One-Way Ride to Nowhere	✓		✓
1944-01-13	Dime a Dance	✓		
1944-01-20	A World of Darkness	✓		
1944-01-27	The Locked Room	✓	✓	✓ see note below
1944-02-03	The Sisters	✓	✓	✓ see note below
1944-02-10	Suspicion	✓		✓
1944-02-17	Life Ends at Midnight		✓	
1944-02-24	Sorry, Wrong Number		✓	✓
1944-03-02	Portrait Without a Face	✓	✓	
1944-03-09	The Defense Rests	✓	✓	
1944-03-16	Narrative About Clarence		✓	
1944-03-23	Sneak Preview	✓		
1944-03-30	Cat and Mouse	✓		
1944-04-06	The Woman in Red	✓		
1944-04-13	The Marvelous Barastro	✓	✓	✓
1944-04-20	The Palmer Method	✓	✓	
1944-04-27	Death Went Along for the Ride	✓		✓

The AFRS versions "The Locked Room" and "The Sisters" are listed in RadioGoldindex but a copies have not been located at this time.

EAST COAST DATE	EPISODE TITLE	EAST (Thurs)	WEST (Mon, 4 days later)	AFRS (source broadcast in paren.)
1944-05-04	The Dark Tower	✓		✓
1944-05-11	The Visitor	✓	✓	
1944-05-18	Donovan's Brain, Part One	✓	✓	
1944-05-25	Donovan's Brain, Part Two	✓		
1944-06-01	Fugue in C-Minor	✓	✓	
1944-06-08	Case History on Edgar Lowndes		✓	
1944-06-15	A Friend to Alexander	✓	✓	✓ *(Thurs)*
1944-06-22	The Ten Grand	✓		
1944-06-29	The Walls Came Tumbling Down	✓		
1944-07-06	The Search for Henri LeFevre	✓	✓	✓
1944-07-13	The Beast Must Die	✓	✓	
1944-07-20	Of Maestro and Man		✓	
1944-07-27	The Black Shawl	✓		
1944-08-03	Banquo's Chair	✓		
1944-08-10	The Man Who Knew How	✓	✓	✓
1944-08-17	The Diary of Sophronia Winters	✓		
1944-08-24	Actor's Blood	✓ "Thursday"	✓ "next week"	
1944-08-31	Black Path of Fear	✓		
1944-09-07	Voyage Through Darkness	✓		
1944-09-14	You'll Never See Me Again	✓		

NOTES:

- It is known that the last Thursday/Monday pair was 1944-09-14 *You'll Never See Me Again*. The *Los Angeles Times* newspaper shows no corresponding West Coast performance on Monday, but the Reno, NV and Santa Cruz, CA newspapers do. It appears that the West Coast had two unique *Suspense* broadcasts that week, the Monday performance of *You'll Never See Me Again* and *Bluebeard of Bellac*. The *Los Angeles Times* shows a *Whistler* broadcast in its listings for the Monday time slot previously used for *Suspense*, which seems to be inaccurate for that day's listing.

- The first week of the new single-day broadcast schedule started on 1944-09-21 with *Bluebeard of Bellac*. There are two versions of the show in circulation, with two different closings. One ends with "Next Thursday, ladies and gentlemen..." and the other ends with "Next Thursday, same time..." This pair of recordings us likely the two performances on that day, one for East, and one for West. *Suspense* aired at 8:00pm in New York (*NY Times*) which would be a 5:00pm Pacific Time studio performance. The show aired at 9:00pm (*LA Times*) in Los Angeles. It is unclear which recording should be associated with which coast.

# # #

The 60-Minute Suspense Episodes: How Roma Left and Auto-Lite Saved the Day

For much of the series, *Suspense* was a sustaining show, but the show had two notable sponsors during its heyday. Roma Wines was the sponsor from December 2, 1943 to November 20, 1947, and Auto-Lite sponsored the program from July 8, 1948 to June 7, 1954.

Suspense switched to an hour-long format in 1948, and for all practical purposes it was an experiment gone bad. The show's ratings had been slipping in 1947 and Roma Wines desired to end its expensive sponsorship, and delayed its cancellation with 13-week contracts after the show won a Peabody Award.

The episode *Dead Ernest* was the one that Peabody judges used in their deliberations. The script had been rejected by William Spier, but his wife, entertainer Kay Thompson, read it and convinced him it was worth doing. The Roma Wines contract was about to be terminated when news of the award arrived. Wine sales were in decline, and Roma's was trying to align their advertising costs to get a reasonable revenue return for their support. That wasn't happening, but the Peabody Award allowed CBS executives to twist the arms of Roma Wines decision-makers into renewal with promises that the publicity would increase listenership. It didn't work out that way.

Just after the announcement that the Roma Wines sponsorship was over, there was speculation that *Suspense* would be canceled. In fact, the November 8, 1947 edition of *Billboard Magazine* stated such with great authority, explaining that the time slot would go to *The FBI in Peace and War*.

There were CBS executives who still wanted the show to continue, and it seems likely that William Paley, head of CBS, led the effort. Based on the news accounts, CBS preferred the half-hour format but had a block of time to fill on Saturday evenings with no satisfactory candidates to fill it.

CBS Wants Chunk Of ABC Crime Aud

With CBS moving "Suspense" (as a sustainer) into the Saturday 8 to 8:55 p.m. stretch, ABC's unbroken lineup of crime shows for that night gets its first challenge from the angle of audience bidding. The sudden assignment of "Suspense" to the spot represents a drastic switch in CBS' program thinking for that night.

It had been Columbia's idea for the past several months to plant a variety show in that span, thereby maintaining an unbroken sequence of that strips through the Joan Davis and Vaughn Monroe shows up to 10 p.m. CBS figured that to give competition to "Life of Riley" and "Truth or Consequence" (8 to 8) on NBC it would have to pose some potent comedy names, and rather than make it variety or novelty with less than top magnets the web elected to rely on a crime show to which it could attach an upper bracket personality, namely, Robert Montgomery

The 1947-12-31 edition of *Variety* indicated that part of the rationale for *Suspense* in its new format was to compete with ABC. Because of its experience with the high ratings of the hour-long *Lux Radio Theatre* series, which drew an audience one-third larger than *Suspense*, some CBS executives believed an hour-long version featuring star actors and actresses could attract a bigger audience, and perhaps a new sponsor. The new format began in January 1948 and featured actor Robert Montgomery along with producer William Spier.

It was probably as last minute a decision one could make in a broadcast network, made more challenging by expanding to a full hour long program. There were no scripts ready for the new format, so they had to scramble and be a bit creative. They lengthened the first 30-minute Roma Wines script from December 1943, *The Black Curtain*. (Was the re-use of this script

an intentional slap of the face of Roma Wines executives?) For
the second week they grabbed a two-year old two-part *Sam
Spade* script, *The Kandy Tooth* and presented it as a one-hour
drama. It was an easy, but probably panicked choice, since
Spade was produced by William Spier. There were many re-used
scripts in the early hour-long format weeks. It was not until the
third week of February that an original script was presented.

They Had Such Good Intentions

At the end of inaugural episode, *Black Curtain*, Montgomery lists
the authors of future productions -- and does not mention
Kandy Tooth as the next week performance. Perhaps that was the
first sign of trouble ahead as an indicator that they had no clue
what they would do next under intense deadline pressure.
Montgomery recited a list prominent authors whose work
would be featured in upcoming programs. They were:

- Marie Belloc Lowndes
- Dashiell Hammett
- Agatha Christie
- Eric Ambler
- John Buchan
- James N. Cain
- Graham Greene
- Raymond Chandler
- Arthur Conan Doyle
- Shakespeare

Only two of those authors works were used in the 60 minute
series:

- James N. Cain - *Love's Lovely Counterfeit*
- Marie Belloc Lowndes - *The Lodger*

You could make a case that Dashiell Hammett was a third

author because of *The Kandy Tooth* performance. But that was not a Hammett story, but Spade was Hammett-created character in a story developed by one of the show's writers.

None of the other authors works were used.

Suspense listeners did hear works of these popular authors in half hour productions over the course of the series (years in parentheses).

Marie Belloc Lowndes	*The Story of Ivy* (1945)
Dashiell Hammett	*Two Sharp Knives* (1942, 1945)
Agatha Christie	*Philomel Cottage* (1942, 1943, 1946), *Where There's a Will* (1949)
John Buchan	*The Thirty-nine Steps* (1952)
Graham Greene	*The Man Within* (1953)
Raymond Chandler	*Pearls are a Nuisance* (1945)
Arthur Conan Doyle	*The Lost Special* (1943)
Shakespeare	*Othello* (1953)

Poor Eric Ambler (not really, he was very successful without *Suspense*): none of his works ended up in *Suspense* whether the show was 60 minutes or 30 minutes. Perhaps they planned his well-known efforts of *Mask of Demitrios* or *Journey Into Fear* (which became an *Escape* production), or another work.

The authors whose works were performed in the 60 minute format authors turned out to be *Suspense* old reliables, and went unmentioned in Montgomery's spoken list: Cornell Woolrich, John Dickson Carr, Curt Siodmak, and Dorothy Sayers, plus some new scripts by different authors.

Suspense did offer Shakespeare's *Othello* as a two-part production under Elliott Lewis. It is not clear if any *Othello* script was in the works for the 60-minute series and if Lewis eventually used that script, if there was one, in the May 1953 production. Collector Keith Scott has information that Spier was planning to produce *Macbeth.*

Behind the Scenes, When No One was Looking...

While *Suspense* was in turmoil at the end of the Roma run and the early hour-long run, William Spier was very busy. His divorce from Kay Thompson was granted, he married actress June Havoc, and jumped from CBS to ABC.

His departure from CBS was likely frustration over creative and management differences, by their indecisiveness and lack of clarity about Montgomery's role as a star producer. According to a materials that Keith Scott has accumulated, Spier had plans to take advantage of the hour-long format with some very ambitious productions of classic mysteries. The details are still being analyzed, but the lack of or slow approval of the network probably played a role in his disgruntled state.

One has to wonder if this path of more classic stories and plays on *Suspense* would have worked as a regular practice. The series always peppered its offerings with classics, but it did the modern dramas so very well.

ABC signed Spier to take over production of their anthology program, *The Clock,* and made a big deal about it in the trade press. In the end, *The Clock* could not be saved, despite Spier's few months at the helm. In that short period, however, he employed the services of some of his most reliable actors and some previous *Suspense* scripts such as *John Barbey and Son* (1945), *House in Cypress Canyon, Can't We Be Friends,* and *Bank Holiday* (1946). It's likely that the CBS executives were not very pleased by this. One episode of *The Clock* would eventually make it to *Suspense* was *Search for Isabel* (1949).

While the Spier sideshow was playing out, *Suspense* was still suffering in its new format. Some news accounts make it seem that Montgomery was being difficult, seeking to be paid separately for being a producer and receiving a duplicate equal payment for the episodes in which he was a cast member. In the meantime, Anton M. Leader started to handle production of the series. (Most OTR fans know Leader as the producer of the 1946 syndicated series *Murder at Midnight*).

Meanwhile, it seems that Paley was letting the Montgomery situation go unresolved while he was negotiating quietly with Auto-Lite, among others, to sponsor *Suspense* in its original half-hour format. It may have been a publicity and internal diversion while he worked on a different strategy for *Suspense*.

Paley's efforts to return to a sponsored half hour may have started as soon as the first hour-long broadcasts were making their debut. One of Paley's objectives was to bundle the sponsorship of the radio series with a new *Suspense* television program. He developed such strong influence over Auto-Lite that he demanded they change advertising agencies, something that is "never" done, and Auto-Lite complied. The deal was done and the Montgomery situation resolved in the process with his resignation. It's likely Paley was never interested in negotiating with Montgomery, and probably never believed the hour format would succeed.

The final hour show was expected to be the April 10, 1948 broadcast, an adaptation of the movie *Crossfire*. It is possible that an adaptation of *Crossfire* was originally intended for *Lux Radio Theatre* since the movie was in theaters at the time, but this adaptation was created by *Suspense* writers.

Suspense continued for a four more episodes, one of which was in a 30-minute format, a re-performance of the script *Life Ends at Midnight*.

Auto-Lite agreed to sponsor the series in its original half-hour format with Leader as the producer. Spier was likely their preferred choice, but he was not available because of his contract for *The Clock* and a contract for the 1949-1950 season of *Philip Morris Playhouse*. For the latter, Spier also used these *Suspense* scripts in the 1949-1950 *Playhouse* season: *Banquo's Chair* (1943), *Diary of Sophronia Winters* (1943), *Cat and Mouse* (1944), *Night Man* (1944), *August Heat* (1945), *Spoils for Victor* (1946), and *Search for Isabel* (1949, which he first used for *The Clock* in 1948). In later years, some *Playhouse* scripts would appear on *Suspense*, notably *Four Hours to Kill* (1950), *One Millionth Joe* (1950), *Lady Killer* (1950), and finally, *Silver Frame* (1958, which Spier authored).

The first Auto-Lite show, broadcast on July 8, 1948 was *The Last Chance*, and starred Cary Grant. The show is missing, but the script exists. That title may have been quite fitting, as without a sponsor, *Suspense* might have withered away, never to return.

The Auto-Lite run would last until mid-1954. It offered some of the series' best episodes, and its lush budget still allowed for big name Hollywood stars to appear on the program. The per-show budget actually increased under Auto-Lite.

Leader's tenure would end with the Summer season in 1949. His efforts resulted in *Suspense* reaching number one in the Hooper ratings just two months into the Auto-Lite sponsorship. Spier would return that September 1949 for one more year as producer with Norman Macdonnell often directing. After Spier's departure, *Suspense* would enter its Elliott Lewis and William N. Robson production eras. Leader would move into television and other projects.

Of the 19 performances in the hour-long *Suspense* era, only 9 were original scripts; the first new script did not appear until the eighth week of the series.

Only 15 true hour long scripts were produced, plus 5 half hour repeat script productions: the two parts of *Kandy Tooth*, and the half-hour scripts of *August Heat*, *Wet Saturday*, and *Life Ends at Midnight*.

Nothing turned out as originally proclaimed at the end of the first hour episode. *Suspense* did survive for another fourteen years, despite the all of the self-imposed chaos in its back rooms.

DATE	TITLE	SOURCE OR DATE OF PREVIOUS BROADCAST
1948-01-03	The Black Curtain	1943-12-02 and 1944-11-30
1948-01-10	The Kandy Tooth	*Adventures of Sam Spade* two-part story from 1946-11-17 and 11-24
1948-01-17	Love's Lovely Counterfeit	1945-03-08
1948-01-24	The Black Angel	*Eve*, 1944-10-19
1948-01-31	Bet with Death	*Will You Make a Bet with Death? 1942-11-10*
1948-02-07	Donovan's Brain	1944-11-18 and 11-25
1948-02-14	The Lodger	1944-12-14
1948-02-21	**Beyond Reason**	**original**
1948-02-28	**The House by the River**	**original**
1948-03-06	**In a Lonely Place**	**original**
1948-03-13	**Nightmare**	**original** (title was reused on 1949-09-01 but different storyline)
1948-03-20	Wet Saturday and August Heat	*Wet Saturday* produced on 1942-06-24, 1943-12-16, and 1947-12-19 and *August Heat* on 1945-05-31
1948-03-27	**Night Must Fall**	**original**; this was a popular play, became a 1937 movie starring Robert Montgomery, and was performed on *Philip Morris Playhouse* and *Screen Guild Theatre*; this *Suspense* episode had its own adaptation, by Robert L. Richards
1948-04-03	Suspicion	1944-02-10
1948-04-10	**Crossfire**	**original**
1948-04-24	**The Search**	**original**
1948-05-01	**The Blind Spot**	**original**
1948-05-08	Life Ends at Midnight (*note: 30 minute program*)	1944-02-17
1948-05-15	**Deadline at Dawn**	**original**

The Search*: The Long-Sought Missing Segment of the Hour-Long Episode*

The Search is a *Suspense* episode written by Grace Amundson. It was produced by Anton M. Leader. It is one of the better hour-long presentations, originally broadcast on April 24, 1948, and is an original script.

The first transcription disc side of the four required to hold an hour-long broadcast is missing, likely broken or unplayable, and unlikely to be found. There were likely four separate discs, recorded on one side only, for this program. Collectors have sought the full recording of this episode for decades. The Armed Forces Radio Service was probably not supplied recordings of the hour-long *Suspense* programs as no AFRS recordings of this *Suspense* era have ever surfaced. That means there is no other source for this missing portion of the program, unless there was an aircheck recording that has yet to emerge. Since the series was sustained at this point, there was no need for an advertiser to request a copy of the performance.

The lack of the story opening has made it hard to grasp the full setting of the episode and the relationship of the characters. The script for the program exists, and a summary is below. If you have heard the episode before, it will probably be worth the time to listen again after reading the summary. If you have never listened to the episode, the summary is essential to its maximum enjoyment.

Bill Johnstone is the voice of *Suspense* and Gil Stratton is the announcer. Stratton also plays a small role in the drama.

Summary of the Story's Opening Scenes, from the Original Script

The setting for the story is in the Dakotas near the Montana border. There are four primary characters , Sid Latch (Howard Culver), Roger Miles (Berry Kroeger), Iris Johnson (Sandra Gair), and Sid's dog named "Bo" (animal imitation specialist Pinto Colvig).

Sid owns a herd of sheep that he has been raising with plans to sell them at market. Sid and Bo have been drifting for quite a long time, and Sid would like to be settled. He wants to establish himself financially by purchasing land of his own with the proceeds from this herd.

There is a severe blizzard with very high winds. Sid is concerned about whether the lambs will survive the night. He will wait out the storm in the safety of his chuck wagon ("food truck" in today's jargon) where he lives.

Sid and Bo hear a car approach. An unknown man, whom we learn is Roger Miles, gets out of the car and calls out. He can barely see Sid and the chuck wagon. Sid tells Roger that his car is stuck because the snow is too high. He tells him to lock the car up and to wait it out. Miles says that he is a little drunk but will wait it out in the chuck wagon. We learn he is a western movie star, Roger Miles.

Sid realizes that there is someone else in the car, Iris Johnson. She says she'd rather stay in the car because Miles can be difficult when he is drunk. Sid says it's not safe to stay in the car and that he and Bo will look after everyone in the wagon. Iris warns him that he is taking in a drunk and a fool. Iris ran away with Miles from her home in Wallace, South Dakota, because "a handsome movie actor whispered in her ear." Miles later admits that he doesn't even know her name. Iris says she wants to go home and Miles says "it's not that easy." It's clear Iris is trapped and fearful of Miles. Miles brags about how easy it is for him to pick up young girls fans, and how many people attend his public appearances.

A belligerent, more drunk Miles asks for dinner. Sid says all that he can offer is fried bread. Miles hears the bleats of the lambs in the distance and insults Sid by saying that cowboys hate sheepherders because the sheep eat away good grassland. Sid asks if Miles is a cowboy, and he says "I am a cowboy" and that Sid doesn't know who he is because he doesn't go out to the movies and that Sid is "cut off from the modern world." Sid says the world seems to go along without him.

The recording picks up at this point of the story, with the drunken Miles antagonizing Sid and Iris with his nasty and belittling banter, which has turned to how much money his celebrity status raised for sale of war bonds.

The missing network ID and break

A little after the 22-minute mark of the current recording there is a network identification. What follows in the script is also missing. At this point, the script reads as follows, read by Bill Johnstone:

> And now back to our Hollywood Sound Stage and Act Two of "THE SEARCH."

> Sid Latch has been alone in the world – except for his dog Bo. Alone on a Dakota prairie with a few head of sheep – and a deep desire to have land of his own. Then came the wind, the

full, ill wind swirling him into active partnership with terror and despair. The wind, pressuring him – blowing him across the wide land that might have been his to own, with panic at his heels and a beautiful girl at his side. When would it end? in a dilapidated little motel on the edge of a strange town?

And now, with Howard Culver as Sid and with Act Two of "The Search," we again to hope to keep you in -- *SUSPENSE*!

Full cast listing

•Sid Latch	Howard Culver
•Roger Miles •Driver	Berry Kroeger
•Iris Johnson	Sandra Gair
•Bo	Pinto Colvig
•Nick •Mac	Lou Krugman
•Al •Constable	Russell Thorsen
•Will •Joe	Doug Young
•Woman •Eadie	Ann Morrison
•Passenger •Pete	Ira Grossel
•Ed •Druggist	Frank Gerstle
•Boy	Gil Stratton

What Kinds of Ratings did Suspense Have?

There is a book of radio program audience sizes that shows the Hooper Ratings for January of most years for the golden age. It just learned it is available for download https://www.americanradiohistory.com/Archive-Bookshelf/History-of-Broadcasting/A-Thirty-Year-History-of-Programs-Summers-1958-HOB.pdf

This chart was prepared from that resource. It shows three major shows, *Suspense*, *Mr. District Attorney*, and *Lux*. For some reason the 1948 rating for *Suspense* is not available, and it might be that the format bounced around and it had weeks where there was no broadcast early that year. We do know that in September of that year there were reports about its big ratings rebound under Auto-Lite sponsorship and producer Tony Leader. *Mr. DA* ratings end with the closing of the network show.

A side note: It is still hard to believe for a series with ratings as big as *Mr. District Attorney* when Jay Jostyn starred that so few of the episodes exist from that time period. Another thing you learn from the ratings was how big *Dragnet* was, replacing *Mr. DA* for many listeners. *Mr. DA* went to television, initially with Jostyn, and there seem to be no kinescopes of that brief series. That was the main reason it is not in the chart's later years. The book excluded syndicated programs from its ratings compilations, so the Ziv *Mr. DA* series that began in 1954 is not included.

The downslide in all radio ratings after about 1949 in favor of

TV is fairly obvious. Compared to other series, *Suspense* had roughly about 2/3 of the ratings of Benny or Fibber in their mid-1940s heyday.

Hooper Ratings for Suspense, Mr. District Attorney, and Lux Radio Theatre

(please note data are not available for all years)

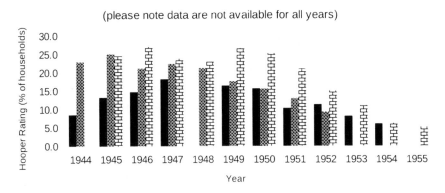

■ Suspense ❈ Mr District Attorney ⊐ Lux Radio Theatre

How to interpret the chart: Data are the percentage of households. During the entire period, the number of households was growing. That means that 10% of households in 1944 is a lot different than 10% of households in 1954 -- the percentage is the same, but the actual number of households is different.

Household formation started to grow at a quicker rate once the troops arrived home from WW2 and civilians went back to their pre-war roles and jobs. In 1944, there were about 37.5 million US households, and by 1955 there were about 48 million. Roughly, in 1947 there were 7 million households tuned into *Suspense* (remember: households, not people) and by 1954 it was down to about 2.8 million households.

Suspense Magazine

The four-edition *Suspense Magazine* is a source of information about the series and about one of the missing single performances, *Fury and Sound*. The magazine was a failed attempt to use the *Suspense* brand in other media. One of the causes, other than poor marketing, was that listeners wanted to hear *Suspense* and not read short story adaptations of the broadcasts. The covers pictured the Hollywood stars who had appeared on the show, but even that kind of magazine rack appeal could not attract readers or advertisers, nor could the assertion that the editor was Leslie Charteris, creator of *The Saint*. This may have been an "in name only" assignment. We suspect the magazine would have been better had Charteris been deeply involved.

There are occasional mistakes on the covers of the magazine that are interesting. The cover of the second issue had two errors, one identifying actor Lee J. Cobb as the lead in *This Was a Hero*. Philip Terry was the actual headliner.

It may have been an innocent editorial mistake, or, the staff may have been working with information from CBS that changed just prior to the final casting. Was Lee J. Cobb the original choice for the role? We may never know.

Cobb's sole appearance on *Suspense* was in 1945's *The Bet*, and Terry made this one appearance. Cobb was on the cover of the first issue for *The Bet*, thus *making more appearances on Suspense magazine covers than he did as a performer!*

The same cover has yet another error, identifying Lucille Ball as starring in *Eve* when that role actually went to Nancy Kelly.

It is not exactly clear how the scripts were selected and how they became short stories. The credits indicated that they were adapted from the scripts; it may have been possible that the editors and writers may have had access to recordings of the programs, but the way the credits are phrased they probably did not.

The contents of the fifth issue were teased in the fourth issue as including the script for *Sorry, Wrong Number*. The magazine never got that far. The other stories that were planned were *Can't We Be Friends*, *Beyond Good and Evil*, *The Westbound Cloud* (adapted from *Westbound Limited* from the 1942 Summer season, a missing show), *I Had an Alibi, My Dear Niece*, and *The Man Who Forgot* (not certain which script this was based on since there is no *Suspense* episode with that title when broadcast).

The short stories based on *Suspense* scripts as they appeared in the magazines have been scanned as PDFs and are available at https://archive.org/details/SuspenseMagazine

List of all *Suspense Magazine* short stories listed by their original broadcast dates

- 1943-08-28 The King's Birthday (issue #2)
- 1943-09-09 Marry for Murder (issue #2)
- 1943-11-02 Statement of Employee Henry Wilson ('Fool Proof' from issue #3)
- 1943-11-16 Thieves Fall Out (issue #2)
- 1943-11-23 Strange Death of Charles Umberstein ('Strange Case of Mark Boren' from issue #4)
- 1944-01-06 One Way Ride to Nowhere ('Ride to Nowhere' from issue #2)
- 1944-01-20 A World of Darkness (issue #3)
- 1944-02-17 Life Ends at Midnight (issue #4)
- 1944-03-02 Portrait Without a Face (issue #1)
- 1944-03-09 The Defense Rests (issue #1)
- 1944-03-23 Sneak Preview (issue #2)
- 1944-04-20 The Palmer Method (issue #1)
- 1944-06-22 Ten Grand (issue #3)
- 1944-07-20 Of Maestro and Man (issue #3)
- 1944-07-27 The Black Shawl (issue #3)
- 1944-09-21 Bluebeard of Belloc ('A Sense of Smell' from issue #4)
- 1944-10-19 Eve (issue #2 - includes error re: Lucille Ball on cover)
- ***1945-07-26 Fury and Sound (issue #1) EPISODE IS MISSING***
- 1945-08-16 Short Order (issue #4)
- 1945-08-23 This Will Kill You ('This'll Kill You' from issue #1)
- 1945-11-08 The Bet (issue #1)
- 1945-11-15 Murder Off Key (issue #4)
- 1945-12-20 Double Entry (issue #3)

- 1946-01-10 This Was a Hero (issue #2 – includes error of Lee J. Cobb on cover)
- 1946-01-47 The Pasteboard Box (issue #3)
- 1946-02-14 Lucky Lady ('Death at Miss Plimm's' from issue #4)
- 1946-03-14 No More Alice (issue #1)
- 1946-08-15 Last Letter of Dr. Bronson (issue #4)

Roma Wines Ad from *Suspense Magazine #2*

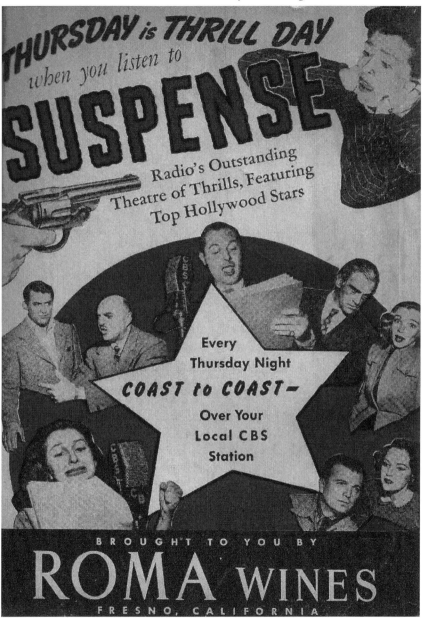

Roma Wines Ad from *Suspense Magazine* #4

Suspense Facts You Never Knew

- The biggest business decision in *Suspense* history may be to have Hollywood stars in lead roles. The first show under the official policy was 1942-12-15 *Til Death Do Us Part* with Peter Lorre. This was key to attracting a national sponsor and lasted until the end of the Auto-Lite era when many stars preferred television work.

- *Suspense* became a big budget show once Roma Wines became the sponsor in late 1943. In 1946, the cost of talent for the show, according to *Billboard Magazine*, was $6,000 per episode. That's $75,000 in today's dollars. Many popular shows, such as *Mr. District Attorney*, had higher ratings and about half the cost. Roma became uncomfortable with the cost and terminated its sponsorship at the end of 1947. When Auto-Lite took over sponsorship in mid-1948, the cost went up to $9,000. This is the equivalent of $92,500 in today's dollars. The bigger budget was evident in the increased production values. Even Auto-Lite became concerned about the costs, and threatened to cancel its deal in 1951. Eventually, in 1954, *Suspense* lost its sponsorship as ad dollars were swiftly moving to television.

- How much did CBS pay for a Suspense script? The March 8, 1943 *Variety* reports that it was $100! That does not seem like a lot, but in 2019 money that's about $1400! It's a pretty good living if you can keep it up and be steady about it, and work your way up to a regular gig.

- In mid-1943 CBS was still looking for a sponsor of *Suspense*. Colgate was reported as interested at the time. The search would not be over until October when Roma Wines signed on.

- *Suspense* inspired a murder? The episode of *The White Rose Murders* of July 6, 1943 was based on the Cornell Woolrich story *The Death Rose* which appeared in the March 1943 issue of *Baffling Detective Mysteries*. This *Suspense* episode is claimed to be the inspiration of a true-life murder! Author Steve Hodel, whose father was the serial killer, details it at his websites.

https://stevehodel.com/2015/10/
maureen-ohara-heroine-of-1943-white-
rose-murders-cbs-radio-broacast-dies-
at-age-95-radio-drama-inspired-dr-
george-hodel-to-commit-real-life-
murder/

There is more detail at this online document starting at about page 5 www.stevehodel.com/wp-content/up loads/2015/01/111.pdf

The Wikipedia entry about the George Hodel murders adds more background

https://en.wikipedia.org/wiki/
George_Hill_Hodel

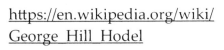

 And this has yet more information...
https://www.theguardian.com/us-news/2016/may/26/black-dahlia-murder-steve-hodel-elizabeth-short

- *Suspense* left for Hollywood in early 1943, but returned to New York for three weeks in 1947. Why? The first reason is that Howard Duff, star of *The Adventures of Sam Spade* needed to be on the set for the filming of the movie *The Naked City*. For those weeks, the *Spade* program's production, under the management of its producer, William Spier, moved to New York. Spier had other reasons to be in town. First, the Roma Wines sponsorship was in trouble, so there were probably lots of meetings with the CBS Radio brass about the problem. Second, soon-to-be wife June Havoc was in a play in Connecticut.

- The June 2, 1943 edition of *Variety* mentions the flub at the end of the first performance of *Sorry, Wrong Number* and that the show will be performed again in a couple of weeks. It wasn't: Agnes Moorehead was not available until August. The very next line of that mentions a young Bruno Zirato, Jr., who, 18 years later, would direct *Suspense* when the show moved back to New York!

> Mexico City for her health....Lucille Fletcher's whodunit script, broadcast May 25 on the 'Suspense' series, will be repeated two weeks hence by CBS because the solution was lost when one of the actors missed a cue in the original performance....Bruno Zirato, Jr., 20-year-old son of the N. Y. Philharmonic Symphony member, will be a student writer this summer with CBS. He's a Columbia University stude....Henry Burbig now di-

- This could have been even stranger had Bruno directed Ms. Moorehead in the eighth and final *SWN* performance, but there was none! CBS replayed the seventh Hollywood performance, directed by William N. Robson, and just edited in new opening and closing announcements that were being used in the New York production at that time.

- In late 1943, Orson Welles performed in a series of episodes for *Suspense*, which may have been a "favor" for William Spier to bring more attention to the new season. In 1933, Spier cast Welles in the program he was producing, *March of Time*. Spier was a broadcast prodigy in that program at age 27, and he thought that Welles was very talented and would have a great career.

- The working title of *Banquo's Chair* was "The Extra Guest." Most *Suspense* know the first performance of the script because it included an apology for the prior week's error in the broadcast of *Sorry, Wrong Number*. Alfred Hitchcock would select *Banquo's Chair* for his television series *Alfred Hitchcock Presents*. That season four, episode twenty-nine was directed by Hitchcock himself. Its unique camera angles, especially its high shots, are still studied today by budding directors.

- In the two-part presentation of *Donovan's Brain*, the sound effect of the brain falling on the floor was created by a bag of wet sand falling into a metal tray. Sound effects pros always came up with ideas like that – but it makes you wonder what else they may have tried.

- The 1945-02-01 episode *Most Dangerous Game* was originally slated to star Cary Grant. This certainly would have had a much different feel to this episode. At the time, Cotten was a favorite high-profile fill-in for *Suspense*.

- The 1945-02-15 episode *Sell Me Your Life* was also supposed to star Grant; Lee Bowman replaced him.

- Two of the biggest Hollywood stars in the mid-1940s were Grant and Gregory Peck. The 1946-03-21 *Lonely Road* stars Peck, but it was originally scheduled for 1946-03-07 with Cary Grant.

- Cary Grant starred in both the inaugural Roma Wines (*The Black Curtain*) and Auto-Lite (*The Last Chance*) shows, almost five years apart. Was his appearance considered to be good luck for a new advertiser? It was probably his wide appeal and ability to attract an audience.

- The most famous script that Cary Grant was expected as star, however, was the highly regarded episode *House in Cypress Canyon* broadcast on 1946-12-05. Robert Taylor replaced him.

- Lloyd Nolan was a replacement in 1945-03-22 *Heart's Desire*. He replaced Richard Whorf. The 1944-06-14 *A Friend to Alexander* and 1944-10-26 *Night Man* ended up being Whorf's only *Suspense* appearances. He may be more famous as a director of TV's *The Beverly Hillbillies*!

- *Two Sharp Knives* may be *Suspense'* unluckiest show. It was scheduled for April 12, 1945, but the death of FDR dominated the radio waves, with nearly all entertainment programs canceled. The show was rescheduled for April 26, but it was canceled again because of news coverage of a multi-day world conference about the formation of the UN in San Francisco. The episode finally came to the air in June, with one of its originally announced stars, John Payne. But Frank McHugh replaced Stuart Erwin. Erwin had been in the 1942 production of this script, and did not appear on *Suspense* at any other time.

- At the end of 1945-01-31 *A Week Ago Wednesday*, the star for next week's *I Won't Take a Minute* was announced as Glenn Ford. But something must have happened between showtime and rehearsals where Ford became unavailable, and Lee Bowman stepped into the part. It was a challenge to keep *Suspense'* Hollywood stars in perfect alignment, because they often scrambled to adjust. Every newspaper listing had Ford in their listings, and not a single one had Bowman. There was obviously not time to "alert the media." If the storyline of *I Won't Take a Minute* sounds familiar, it's because it was repeated on *Escape* as *Finger of Doom*. That was the original title of the Cornell Woolrich novel adapted for the episode.

- Actor Paul Henreid, famous for playing Victor Laszlo in *Casablanca*, had only one appearance on *Suspense* for 1946-03-14 *No More Alice*. His appearance was a last minute change as the original casting was for George Brent. He was a very busy actor, and was seen in movies such as *The Affairs of Susan* (1945), *The Spiral Staircase* (1946), and *Tomorrow Is Forever* (1946). Brent never appeared on *Suspense*, and was never scheduled again. The bulk of his radio appearances were on *Lux Radio Theatre*. Henreid had appeared just a few weeks earlier on *Suspense* in 1946-01-03 *Angel of Death*.

- For years, *Suspense* tried to get Frank Sinatra as a guest star. He was scheduled a few times and it did not work out. The episode that finally got him on the air was *To Find Help* of 1945-01-18. The program was originally planned to air in the previous September. That was probably not a very good time to be on the air for Frank.

  Sinatra had been in California since the Spring of 1944, part of which was to film *Anchors Aweigh* for its 1945 release. Frank seemed to have problems with his experiences in Hollywood, and he vented to a reporter around Labor Day that he was done with the film business. This was, of course, the kind of news that the celebrity magazines and gossip columns loved. He later walked back those comments since he still had a movie contract that had to be fulfilled. He went back to New York but planned to return, and *To Find Help* was scheduled for November 30. That didn't work out for an unknown reason, so *Suspense* aired another performance of *The Black Curtain* with Cary Grant instead. Finally, Sinatra appeared for his only time on *Suspense* in January, 1945.

- The episode of 1957-11-24 *Star Of Thessaly* starred bandleader Ray Noble. At the beginning of the episode, producer William N. Robson claims that it was a new script, written especially for Noble. It's actually a reused script from the Mutual series *The Modern Adventures of Casanova* produced by Robson five years earlier!

- *The Story of Ivy* 1945-06-21 was originally scheduled for 1945-05-03. The latter date's *Suspense* episode was *Fear Paints a Picture* instead. Lana Turner was originally cast for *Story of Ivy* for the May date, as well as *Fear*. There was obviously a change in plans. *Ivy* ended up broadcast on 1945-06-21 with Ann Richards as star. Either *Story of Ivy* was not a good fit for Turner or it wasn't ready.

- In 1945, William Spier was asked to produce Dick Powell's new show, *Rogue's Gallery* but remained with *Suspense*. By 1946, Spier was producing *Sam Spade* as well as *Suspense*. Powell was one of the most talented performers in Hollywood, and a long-term Spier-Powell combination would have been fascinating. Their only *Suspense* collaboration was 1950-02-23 *Slow Burn*.

- While other performers appeared live on *Suspense*, Joan Crawford insisted in appearing only if the show was pre-recorded. The announcing was done live, and the body of the performance was played from transcriptions.

- The original title for *The Thirteenth Sound* was *Dying is Safer*. It's the only episode that was jointly written by actress Cathy and producer Elliott Lewis. Their work in the medium was so prolific, broad, and constant that they were often referred to as "Mr. and Mrs. Radio."

- There is a belief that 1951-12-03 *Murderous Revision* was to star Howard Duff, but he was replaced by Richard Widmark because of his mention in the Communist scare publication *Red Channels*. That was not true. Duff's career was fine. He and producer Elliott Lewis became good friends while doing work for Armed Forces Radio. When Lewis needed someone to sit in at a *Suspense* rehearsal, he often called Duff to a read part even if he wasn't in the cast. Duff and Ida Lupino were newly married, starting their new life together and traveling around that time. Their honeymoon in San Francisco a couple of months before was brief and involved working. They did eventually have a true vacation in December in Mexico, and that may have played a role in re-casting and scheduling.

- There is another possible *Murderous Revision* explanation, or at least another issue that compounds the intrigue. There was an early script with the title *The Twist is Murder* for which the drama portion may have been recorded with Duff months before, in January 1951. The problem was that Duff broke his leg in late 1950, not many weeks after he ended his lead role in the *Adventures of Sam Spade, Detective*. The gossip columns had a field day covering his injury, with one of the accounts being that it was retribution for a gambling debt, or a fall down the stairs when he was "tipsy," and all of the attention he was getting from Hollywood starlets who would visit to "help" him recover. There were even stories about the big argyle sock he wore over the cast as he visited restaurants on crutches. In all that time, he was signing for movie roles, one of which was a western. The machinations around *Murderous Revision* remain very curious and still appear to be much different than the common assertion that he was involved in any *Red Channels* hysteria.

- There was always a great desire to get Alfred Hitchcock on radio to lend his name and reputation to a mystery series, starting with the 1940 CBS *Forecast* series that dramatized *The Lodger* and had an actor imitate

Hitchcock as part of the show. Hitchcock's motion picture success was always an obstacle in his availability and probably in financial negotiations. At the end of 1946, news about a Hitchcock appearance on *Suspense* in early 1947 was reported by Louella Parsons. A deal must have been made, because Hitchcock was announced as an upcoming guest star at the end of 1946-12-26 *Philomel Cottage*. The intent was for him to be part of the small cast of *The Waxwork*. He must not have been available, because the role went to Claude Rains (that recording is missing). What is very funny, however, is the announcement of Hitchcock's potential appearance at the end of the east coast broadcast of *Philomel*. There, Bill Johnstone flubs Hitchock's name, referring to him as "Alexander... (long and uncomfortable pause)... HITCHCOCK!" Announcer Ken Niles can barely read his closing lines properly, holding back his chuckle over Morrison's saying "Alexander" instead of "Alfred." The announcement is correct for the west coast broadcast.

- Arch Oboler, famous for *Lights Out*, on a *Suspense* program? Yes, according to the April 13, 1949 *Variety*. He submitted *Him or Me* for consideration, it was scheduled but not used. It would not be performed until 1964, in his *Arch Oboler's Plays* syndicated series.

- Jimmy Stewart was a beloved Hollywood actor whose appearances on *Suspense* always received a lot of publicity. On 1946-02-21_he appeared in *Consequence*. The original title of the script was *Revenge*. The contract for his performance is available online; he was paid $4,000. That's $49,800 in today's dollars!

Jimmy Stewart's Contract to Appear on *Suspense*

File James Stewart env

The Biow Company, Inc.
9 Rockefeller Plaza
New York, 20, New York

January 01, 1946

2/29/46

Gentlemen:

I hereby agree to perform on the _____ program to be broadcast from a studio in the Columbia Broadcasting System from 8:00 PM to 8:30 PM and rebroadcast from 9:00 PM to 9:30 PM

It is understood and agreed that you and/or your client shall be permitted to use my name, likeness and/or photograph in any way you see fit in connection with the advertising and/or publicizing of this program, but such use shall not be in the nature of an endorsement.

It is understood and agreed that I shall fully cooperate with you in the preparation, design, construction and presentation of my spot on the program, and that I shall not improvise, extemporize or use unapproved material. I further agree to appear in or present all or any part of the commercial announcements or dialogue on this program, including personal testimonials, if I am requested to do so.

It is understood and agreed that I shall be present at all necessary rehearsals which you may reasonably require.

It is understood and agreed that I will not appear on any other radio program between February 1, 194 and March 7, 194.

It is understood and agreed that you are to pay me and I shall receive as full compensation for the services rendered by me hereunder the sum of Four thousand ($4000.00) Dollars, payable to M. C. A. who is my agent, within two week following the broadcast.

Insofar as any of the terms and conditions hereof fail to conform to the minimum applicable requirements of the Code of Fair Practice of the American Federation of Radio Artists now in effect, said minimum requirements shall be deemed controlling. I agree that I am a member in good standing of the American Federation of Radio Artists and shall remain a member in good standing during and throughout the aforementioned engagement hereunder.

I represent and warrant that I am under no contract or other obligation which will prevent me from fulfilling the obligations under this agreement and that if under any outstanding agreement or other obligation I am required to obtain consent or approval for the fulfillment of my obligations hereunder, I represent and warrant that such approval has been obtained.

The singular pronoun as used herein shall include and apply to the plurals of said pronoun and to all genders wheresoever the context hereof will so admit.

Special: (nothing)

Agreed to and Accepted:
THE BIOW COMPANY, INC.

By:

Artist's Social Security No.

Very truly yours,

(JAMES STEWART)

Approved

By:
(Agents)

The website www.jimmystewartontheair.com has recordings and insight into Stewart's career, including this document.

- *Plan X* starred Jack Benny as a Martian who meets the first rocket from earth. For some reason, there is an AFRS recording of it with the title *Strange Disappearance of XY272B*, which was the subtitle of the story. Why the AFRS production personnel edited out "Plan X" as the title will never be known.

- The episode *Two Platinum Capsules* of 1956-01-10 was originally titled *Two Platinum Needles*. It may have been changed because of the possibility of the story being mistaken as about drug addiction, an important social topic of the time. Just a month before the episode, a movie that featured addition opened in theaters. It was *Man with the Golden Arm* starring Frank Sinatra. The *Suspense* story was actually about radiation.

- The *Marvelous Barastro* was a showcase for Orson Welles. It was based on a Ben Hecht short story, *The Shadow*. That's interesting, of course, because Welles did play the radio character *The Shadow* years before, but there was no connection to this character. In Hecht's short story the magician is named "Sarastro." Welles was so pleased with the story that he planned to buy rights to the script and turn it into a movie. That never happened.

- Why did *Suspense* repeat performances of scripts? As the series was coming to its final years, new performances of prior scripts was often a cost-saving measure. The audiences changes over twenty years, but especially in the 1950s when television became the primary medium in US homes. *Sorry, Wrong Number* would be repeated because it was a legendary broadcast. *Dead Ernest* was repeated when it won a Peabody Award, but repeats were selected because they were good scripts. The Spier years had another reason: the planned guest star suddenly became unavailable. *Suspense* guest slots were important but sometimes sudden demands for motion picture production took precedence. When a filming schedule changed, the *Suspense* commitment would need to be broken. When the planned guest star's schedule changed, Spier had some favorites as emergency replacements, especially Joseph Cotten. Spier would also be sure to pick a script that the substitute star may have performed before (such as Cary Grant and *Black Curtain* in Fall 1944). In this way, the production staff and the actors could get ready for the broadcast more easily. Research of industry publications and newspaper articles indicate that coordinating guest appearances usually took at least six to eight weeks in advance of the intended broadcast date. Those weeks were often chaotic and full of surprises. The public, however, had no hint of what it was like behind the scenes as *Suspense* delivered on its entertainment promise week after week.

- Liza Minelli has a special connection to *Suspense* – and the episode *Drive-In*. Judy Garland was close friends with producer William Spier and his then-wife, Kay Thompson. They became godparents of Liza, and convinced Judy to appear on *Suspense*. Garland was originally reluctant to do so. Thompson became Liza's mentor for her career.

- Kay Thompson's influence on *Suspense* was significant. In the superb biography of her, *Kay Thompson: From Funny Face to Eloise* by Sam Irvin. It's clear that she pulled *Dead*

Ernest from the rejected scripts pile (it ended up getting *Suspense* its Peabody award), encouraged the performing-against-type where musical performers appeared in dramatic roles, assisted in the recruiting of MGM stars to make *Suspense* appearances, and probably much more. Most importantly, she opined that *Sorry, Wrong Number* would be more effective if the script eliminated the original ending of police rescuing Mrs. Stevenson from her killer and replaced it with her murder. That ending was so opposite of listener expectations that the show became a legend, a movie, a stage play, a book, a television production, and… an opera! (see the special *SWN* chapter of this book). Irvin's book is exceptional, with lots of detail about *Suspense*. Be sure to look at the

"endnotes" website Irvin set up with an incredible amount of information that was too granular for inclusion in the book. The PDF file is at http://www.kaythompsonwebsite.co m/index_htm_files/ENDNOTES_1_20 18.pdf

- Speaking of *Dead Ernest*, the plot of a cataleptic who seems dead but is alive is not so outlandish. On January 9, 2018, the website *Live Science* had an article "Man Declared Dead Snores to Life Right Before His Autopsy." A Spanish prisoner snored just four hours after he had been declared dead by three forensic specialists. https://www.livescience.com/61385-man-declared-dead-really-alive.html If you're a cataleptic, be sure to carry a note about it with you, and don't lose it the way Ernest did!

- Producer William N. Robson (October 1956 to August 1959) was known for his personal introduction of each episode. He was the only producer or director to speak on the program regularly. Excepting Elliott Lewis and Antony Ellis who appeared on the series as actors, the voice of the producer was rare on *Suspense*. William Spier can be heard on the (missing) *Fury and Sound*, 1946-09-12 *Hunting Trip*, 1947-12-26 *Too Little to Live On*, and on the first hour-long episode 1948-01-03 *The Black Curtain*.

- Spier's soon-to-be wife, June Havoc, appeared on *Suspense* often, and not always credited. She appeared on the show as "Armona Fargay" on 1947-11-13 *ioboushinska*. In the 1947-11-20 *One Hundred in the Dark*, she is billed as "Theresa Marshall." They would marry in February 1948.

- There were other pseudonyms used on *Suspense*, including Mason Adams as "Matt Cooper" and Hy Averback as "Joel Samuels." The use of pseudonyms, aside from occasional harmless mischief among the cast, was often a solution to a contract conflict where the actor agreed not to have on-air credit for their performance.

- It was no secret in the back rooms that *Suspense* original producer Charles Vanda and star producer William Spier did not get along. The friction began when Vanda returned from WW2 and his role in creating and managing the Armed Forces Radio Service. Vanda expected to return to *Suspense*, but Spier would not let go. If the tense relationship started there, it only got worse.

In a small item in 1954-04-07 *Variety* about new television programs going into production, Spier was cited as "the originator" of *Suspense*. Upon reading that, an angry Vanda sent a telegram, citing the article, and stating:

> This is a base canard. I launched it in Hollywood on *Forecast* in 1939 and started the series in 1941. No other director or producer had anything to do with it until I went into the Army in 1942. Spier asked if he could do it while I was overseas and I said yes, which was my biggest mistake. You can print this wire if you wish.

Vanda ended up having a spectacular career, especially in owning and selling TV stations while still being involved in production. Through the years, Spier and Vanda's relationship got worse. There is no doubt that Vanda "founded" *Suspense*. But he also produced it as a British-style mystery series with plodding plots and spooky stories. Spier turned it into a franchise of exceptional production values with "people in trouble" or "things are not what they seem" storylines rather than dark mysteries. It was sad to learn of their rift and how played out over the years. Spier died in his late 60s, but Vanda lived well into his 80s and was still very, very active in the arts and philanthropy, doing what he enjoyed, until his passing.

- "Red Mountain" may have been a favorite name for some reason on *Suspense*. The episode *Snow on 66* takes place on "Red Mountain." And then, of course, the episode *Nobody Ever Quits* was repeated twice more, with the title *Night on Red Mountain*!

- *The Man Who Threw Acid*, broadcast on 1955-07-18, is a "ripped-from-the-headlines" story. On the evening of

April 5, 1956, labor reporter and commentator Victor Riesel was blinded by an assailant hurling sulfuric acid. Riesel had campaigned against corruption in labor union and the activities of the Communist party in the US labor movement. Riesel was assisting the U.S. District Attorney of New York's probe into labor racketeering. He was held in very high esteem by rank and file workers as he was on their side while years of union corrupt practices were in the courts and in the news. The attack received nationwide coverage. The *Suspense* episode, "loosely" based on the Reisel incident was planned for May 1, less than a month after it happened. The script, by Antony Ellis, was changed it to the numbers racket and a political figure, but everyone knew what the plot was based on. The broadcast was delayed, but the television version of *The Big Story* broadcast their true-to-life version on June 14. The *Suspense* broadcast was still delayed, but finally scheduled for July 11. It was delayed again, replaced by *Want Ad*. It finally aired on July 18. Reisel's attackers were not apprehended until August.

- Mel Dinelli was a prolific and successful radio and movie scriptwriter *(The Spiral Staircase*, and others*)*, but Auto-Lite rejected a script he had written for his occasional social companion, Joan Crawford. *The Hand* was one of the few scripts to be turned down for being objectionable. The story concerned a woman who involved in an auto accident. When she gets to the other car she discovers the driver's severed hand, and it was still clutching an envelope filled thousands of dollars in cash. She takes the money, puts it in a purse, and is soon haunted by obsessive thoughts of the hand. She believes the hand is still in the purse, and during the trial she breaks down with fear of the purse being opened. The image of the hand in the purse was in her mind, affected by her narcotic addiction. Two things may have turned Auto-Lite off, the car accident and the narcotics. Dinelli did sell the screenplay rights in 1956, but it seems the movie was never made.

- Hollywood stars appeared on *Suspense* and sometimes all seemed well in their lives. In the case of Leon Ames (*An Evening's Diversion*, 1946-07-04), the story of what happened to him is so strange, it seems to come out of a *Suspense* plot. Ames was a successful character actor and one of the founders of the Screen Actors Guild in 1933. At the time of his *Suspense* appearance, he was popular for his role in *The Postman Always Rings Twice*. He and his wife were victims of a kidnapping in 1964, foiled by the actions of his business partner. The story gets stranger. The criminal, Lynn Wayne Benner, was convicted and sent to Folsom prison. Benner escaped in 1970 and attempted another home invasion, but failed and returned to Folsom, his victims unharmed. A few years later, his cellmate would be Dr. Timothy Leary of LSD fame. They would become friends and talk about a range of things including interstellar travel, UFOs, and ESP. They tried to escape Folsom via levitation (it didn't work).

- There is a book about *Suspense* that contends that Orson Welles wrote scripts for the series, especially *Marvelous Barastro*, and others, under a pen name of "Jacques Finke." It's not true. Jack Finke was a real person. Finke also adapted *One Hundred in the Dark* for *Suspense*. He also did some movie studio script work, editing those of others and writing his own, but working in the background in usually low profile positions in studios as well as freelancing.

- Who turned out the lights when *Suspense* and *Yours Truly, Johnny Dollar* ceased broadcast on September 30, 1962? The best candidate may be Jack Johnstone, who wrote the scripts used on both shows that day. *Devilstone* was performed on *Suspense* under his pen name of Jonathan Bundy, and *The Tip-Off Matter* was written under his own name.

- *Suspense* was canceled three times that we know about. First, in 1947 when the Roma Wines was not renewed. Second, on November 25, 1960, when CBS canceled its soap operas, with *Suspense* caught in the undertow. The idled New York actors and studios were switched to *Yours Truly, Johnny Dollar*, which moved from Hollywood at that time. It was somewhat of a surprise when *Suspense* appeared in 1961 as a replacement for *Gunsmoke*. Then, finally, the axe permanently fell on September 30, 1962. That final cancellation was rumored for months in *Variety* and other trade publications. In fact, many of the articles point to initial discussions about ending radio drama in 1959!

- William Spier penned four scripts used in *Suspense*. The only one he produced was *Summer Storm* (1945-10-18). *Death and Miss Turner* (1952-11-16 produced by Lewis and 1957-05-19 by Robson), *Man Alive* (1952-11-24 by Lewis), and *Silver Frame* (1958-02-02 by Robson).

- The loss of a sponsor meant that the relationships of cast and crew would likely be changing and some members would be let go, or the program would be canceled. For Auto-Lite's final sponsored program, *Terribly Strange Bed,* broadcast 1954-06-07, announcer Harlow Wilcox's voice breaks at about 28:00. He's reading the closing copy of *Suspense* likely for the last time after many years, but he does hold it together. His *Fibber McGee and Molly* announcing gig ended the previous year.

- There were nine Lucille Fletcher scripts used on *Suspense,* with four having repeat performances, leading to a total of 21 broadcasts.

Title	Broadcasts
Sorry, Wrong Number	8
Diary of Sophronia Winters	3
Night Man	3
The Thing in the Window	2
The Hitch-hiker	1
Fugue in C Minor	1
Search for Henri Lefevre	1
The Furnished Floor	1
Dark Journey	1

- Sound effects artist Ross Murray was "fired" for one night, 1951-12-17, because his script *Case History of a Gambler* was being performed. Elliott Lewis thought he would be too nervous about the event to work that day.

- Eleazar Lipsky was one of the more fascinating writers for *Suspense.* He was an assistant district attorney in Manhattan in the 1940s and had a successful law career, but he was most known by the public was as a successful novelist. His most famous work is the story that was adapted to become the movie *Kiss of Death,* for which he received an Academy Award nomination. A movie based on his novel *The People Against O'Hara was* adapted for *Lux Radio Theatre* on 1953-03-09; an *AFRS Hollywood Theater* version exists. There were three *Suspense* episodes written by him, *Infanticide* 1959-10-11, this episode of *The Thimble*, and *End of the Road* 1960-01-31. His title of the latter is a different story than the 1947-02-06 *Suspense* program of the same title. Lipsky's *End of the Road* was actually a re-used script, originally performed on *Indictment*, a late 1950s CBS series held in high regard but of which there are very few episodes in circulation.

- When *Suspense* moved back to New York around Fall 1959, the show began to use New York actors and writers. One of those writers was Robert Arthur whose work was featured on *The Mysterious Traveler* and *The Sealed Book*. The Suspense script *The Man Who Went Back to Save Lincoln* was originally broadcast as *The Man Who Tried to Save Lincoln* on *The Mysterious Traveler* on February 7, 1950. One actor appeared in both of the productions, and that was Ralph Bell. *The CBS Radio Mystery Theater* of September 26, 1975, *Assassination in Time*, also dealt with a trip back to Lincoln's time. That script was written by Ian Martin, star of this *Suspense* episode.

- Other *Mysterious Traveler* scripts on *Suspense* were likely, among possible others, the ones identified to date are:
  - 1944-08-20 *Time on My Hands*, used 1960-09-25
  - 1950-01-24 *A Dead Man's Story*, used 1960-05-15
  - 1950-05-09 *The Big Dive*, used 1960-08-07
  - 1951-03-20 *A Coffin for Charley* was probably *A Coffin for Mr. Cash* of 1960-03-27
  - 1952-03-18 *The Black Door*, used 1961-11-19

East and West: When Did *Suspense* have Separate Live Performances for the Coasts?

The challenge of being a growing country with three time zones and a show that audiences love is making sure as many of them have a chance to hear it. For that reason, many of radio's best shows had two live performances on the night they were scheduled. *Suspense* was one of them, but their duplicate East-West performances did not last very long.

Documenting how long that period lasted required an examination of scripts and newspaper timetables. Luckily that kind of research is much easier today than it was before.

This is verified: Suspense *had separate live performances for the east and west only when the series was sponsored by Roma Wines.*

As soon as Roma canceled with their last sponsored episode *One Hundred in the Dark*, the production schedule went to a single live performance broadcast nationally.

During the Roma years, there was usually a 5:00pm Pacific live performance that would be heard in the East at 8:00pm. The cast would break and then return <u>four</u> hours later for a 9:00pm Pacific live performance.

For the time of the one hour episodes run and the Auto-Lite run, there were single live national performances. The hour long episodes were on Saturday nights in the East at 8:00pm and at 5:00pm in the West, all live.

When Auto-Lite started in Summer 1948, it was at the same times.

Technology played a role in seasons starting in the 1951-1952 season as a shift was made to have delayed playback for the West. That coast started to hear a recorded *Suspense* at a much better time. The live performances were at 5:00pmPT and were heard in the East at 8:00pmET. The West would hear their playback at a more reasonable time, 9:00pmPT.

CBS was also recording drama portions of many of their programs separately, allowing for edits and also flexible scheduling of performing and production talent. This was especially useful for series with regular characters and cast members.

Suspense appears to have a strong preference for live performances, and they did not adopt prerecorded drama portions of their episodes as a standard procedure, but used it when necessary or appropriate. *Suspense* was an anthology, so the requirements for production were different.

From examining the scripts of this period, the prerecording was based on the availability or negotiated requirement of the guest. In the review of scripts, the process was used for Milton Berle, Jack Benny, and others. Joan Crawford was not comfortable appearing on live radio, so this was the approach used for her performance. There is no other pattern of using this production method that I was able to discern, but further study may change this observation. *Suspense* was still a high class radio performance destination, so its producers could make the rules for guests and bend those rules for top billed stars and their movie studios whenever they felt necessary.

A good example is the missing episode *Deadline,* starring Broderick Crawford. He had won an Oscar and was in high demand. The *Deadline* script cover indicates that they rehearsed and recorded the drama portions *on a Saturday night starting at 7:00pm*, twelve days before the broadcast. On broadcast day, the orchestra and announcing personnel would appear in-person and do their jobs while the transcription was playing.

It all changed again when the Auto-Lite contract expired. Everything became recorded in advance, even if it was a day before broadcast. Because there was lesser emphasis on Hollywood stars and greater reliance on radio performers, schedules were changed. When recording tape was adopted by *Suspense* in late 1956, there was greater flexibility in the scheduling.

How East and West Coast Recordings be Identified?

Sometimes it's hard, and sometimes it's easy, and sometimes it can't be done.

Some shows have in-show identifiers, such as referring to a program that is only on the schedule in that area. In the case of airchecks, listen for that station's ID at the end of the program.

The only other way to identify east and west is by having the transcriptions with their original labels for verification and being sure that the file names for the digital recordings properly designate the recording. There are many shows in circulation that were recorded from transcriptions and the east-west status is noted in the file names. We appreciate the thoroughness of those collectors in documenting that source.

We have developed a habit of listening to the ends of programs for the new recordings we find, and compare them with the recordings we already have. In many cases, we have identified recordings where the network ID (as in "This is the Columbia Broadcasting System") is at a different pace or specific time than the dialogue that precedes it. We have two different recordings each of *Blue Eyes* and *Story of Ivy* where one has an obvious rush to the network ID and the other has a normally paced expression of it, usually after some music.

There are other recordings such as *Three Blind Mice* where one recording has "Will the defendant rise" after the commercial while another recording has "Does the defendant wish to make a statement." Other recordings have different opening announcements, such as "The Roma Wines Company of Fresno, California" while another for the same script has "Now… Roma Wines present…"

There's only one problem with these differences: we have no idea which is east or west, just that they are different separate performances.

For a time in the Roma Wines sponsorship, there is a special in-show identifier that is very specific and very definite.

From August 23, 1945 through August 7, 1947, *FBI in Peace and War* followed Suspense in the East and Central time zones. *FBIiP&W* did not have a repeat performance, just a national one. Many *Suspense* broadcasts, if there was still time in the program, urged East listeners to stay tuned for *FBIiP&W*. Hearing this indicates that this was an East broadcast, definitively. If there is no mention, it can be either East or West, because the announcement could be left out if the director believed time was running out. This image shows how the text usually appeared in the script.

NILES: Produced and directed by William Spier for the Roma Wine Company of Fresno, California.

(EARLY SHOW ONLY)

Stay tuned for the thrilling adventures of the FBI in Peace and War, followed immediately over most of these stations.

Note how it's referred to as the "early show," with no mention of geography affected. The announcement usually was made in the very last moments of the broadcast, but it has been heard earlier depending on where the concluding Roma Wines commercial was in the script.

When you listen to *Suspense* episodes that are from that August 1945 to August 1947 period, please keep an ear out for the announcement, and let us know if it's an addition to what we have found so far.

This is the list of recordings that are in circulation that we can definitely state are "early" recordings for the East:

- 1946-10-31 Lazurus Walks EC (mentions FBIiP&W)
- 1946-11-07 Easy Money EC (mentions FBIiP&W)
- 1946-12-19 Thing In The Window EC (mentions FBIiP&W)
- 1946-12-26 Philomel Cottage EC (mentions FBIiP&W)
- 1947-01-09 Will to Power EC (mentions FBIiP&W) EC
- 1947-01-16 Overture In Two Keys EC (mentions FBIiP&W)
- 1947-02-20 Always Room At The Top EC (mentions FBIiP&W)
- 1947-02-27 Three Faces At Midnight EC (mentions FBIiP&W)
- 1947-04-03 Swift Rise Of Eddie Albright EC (mentions FBIiP&W)
- 1947-04-24 Win Place and Murder EC (mentions FBIiP&W)
- 1947-05-01 Lady In Distress EC (mentions FBIiP&W)
- 1947-05-15 Death At Live Oak (EC mentions FBIiP&W)
- 1947-05-22 Knight Comes Riding EC (mentions FBIiP&W)
- 1947-06-19 Dead Of Night EC (mentions FBIiP&W)
- 1947-07-24 Murder By An Expert EC (mentions FBIiP&W)

Suspense in the Movies

Sorry, Wrong Number is obviously the most famous *Suspense* script that became a movie. There were many *Suspense* scripts that were considered for motion picture release, but very few made it that far. Many of the movies play on Turner Classic Movies cable channel. Some did make it to the silver screen

- *Argyle Album* was retitled *Argyle Secrets* and became a B-movie in its release in 1948.

The IMDb details can be found at https://www.imdb.com/title/tt0040112/

It can be viewed on YouTube
https://www.youtube.com/watch?
v=k7K319JJnsc

The movie includes actors more familiar to television audiences, such as William Gargan (radio's Barrie Craig, and early TV's Martin Kane), Marjorie Lord (*Make Room for Daddy*), John Banner (Sgt. Schultz of *Hogan's Heroes*), and Barbara Billingsley (Mrs. Cleaver on *Leave it to Beaver*). It's claimed that it was filmed in eight days!

- *One Way Ride to Nowhere* was released in 1946 as *Last Crooked Mile*. The IMDb page for this B-movie is at https://www.imdb.com/title/tt0038683

None of the lead players are notable, but playing a gangster is one of radio's greatest voices, John Dehner (*Have Gun Will Travel, Frontier Gentleman*). There are copies available through online sellers now and then, but they are hard to find. The movie is often shown at *film noir* festivals.

- *Cabin B-13* was released as *Dangerous Crossing* in 1953. Its IMDb page is at http://www.imdb.com/title/tt0045669/ The movie can sometimes be found at YouTube but it is usually removed because it is available as a studio-release DVD.

Its trailer can be viewed at archive.org https://archive.org/details/DangerousCrossingTrailer

- *To Find Help* was a play (*The Man*) prior to its *Suspense* broadcast. It became a movie *Beware, My Lovely* in 1952, starring Ida Lupino. The IMDb listing is at https://www.imdb.com/title/tt0044417.

The film is not available on DVD, but was released on VHS tape. A trailer can be seen on YouTube https://www.youtube.com/watch?v=Ti_A50yir_4

- One *Suspense* program, *The Walls Came Tumbling Down*, was a novel prior to its appearance on the series. The movie is available on DVD. It was released in 1946 and its IMDb information can be found at https://www.imdb.com/title/tt0039094/

- **Black Path of Fear** was based on a Cornell Woolrich story and became the movie *The Chase*. The movie starred Robert Cummings and Michelle Morgan. https://www.imdb.com/title/tt0038409/?ref =fn tt tt 10

  The movie can be viewed on YouTube.

  https://youtu.be/y9T0mEtpeqQ

- The 1942 movie *Street of Chance* is based on the same Cornell Woolrich story as the episode **The Black Curtain**. It stars Burgess Meredith and Claire Trevor. https://www.imdb.com/title/tt0035388/?ref_=nm_flmg_wr_100

Suspense producer William Spier tried his hand in movie direction with 1952's *Lady Possessed* starring his wife, June Havoc, and James Mason. The screenplay was by Pamela Mason. The movie is available on DVD. The IMDb page is at https://www.imdb.com/title/tt0044817

Suspense on Broadway? *The Visitor* became a Broadway play. The show had 23 performances; its Playbill is at http://www.playbill.com/production/the-visitor-henry-millers-theatre-vault-0000013542.

The First Summer of *Suspense*, 1942

Suspense began as a summer replacement series. The show did not have a lot of publicity prior to its opening, and newspapers did not give it much coverage on a week-to-week basis.

The first episode, *The Burning Court* received a harsh review in *Variety's* 1942-06-24 edition. The show was not considered anything special. Some of the newspaper listings would not even list the episodes as *Suspense*, but would just generically list it as "play" or "drama." The show did not have its "brand" yet.

The early shows set the tone as a British-style drama with influence from author. This period of the series is not held in high regard by *Suspense* fans, but everyone realizes that the series was just getting its bearings.

Many of the programs are missing and newspaper information when available is sketchy and often

'SUSPENSE'
With Charles Ruggles, Julie Haydon, Bob Emery, Ted Osborne, Irene Winston
Mystery Drama
30 Mins.
Sustaining
Wednesday, 10:30 p.m.
WABC-CBS, New York

Columbia has taken up here where it left off last summer. The 'Suspense' framework was part of the 'Forecast' group of sample programs. The thing that marked the presentation of the mystery item last summer was the attachment of Alfred Hitchcock's name to the piece for publicity purposes. Hitchcock was supposed to be the producer, but when rehearsals were called in Hollywood the film megger was in New York enjoying his favored two-inch steaks. Charles Vanda produced the sample 'Suspense' and the job that came out of CBS' studios last week by way of New York was also performed by him. It was okey-doke entertainment but nothing to get especially excited about.

For the revival of the 'Suspense' idea as a regular series the Columbia producing menage could have chosen a better opening fable. John Noxon Carr's story, 'The Burning Corpse,' didn't lend itself to the sort of adaptation that makes the most out of radio's peculiar technique. Both the scripter, Harold Medford, and the producer appeared to have no little difficulty keeping the skeins of the narrative from getting entangled. At times it was rather hard on the listener to keep the numerous characters properly indexed. The plot had to do with a femme poisoner, the theory of reincarnation, on empty crypt and the stupidity of a guy who knew he was dealing with a Lucretia Borgia but who qualified the mickey anyway.

Cast credits over the air were limited to Charles Ruggles and Julie Haydon. Ruggles, who was described as a comedian whose craving to play a deadly serious role was herein being fulfilled, gave a sharply defined performance in the character of the author with a yen for poisoning cases. The mechanical device was the now common form of having a narrator dominate the unfoldment and the action being intersliced between his first-person comments. Ruggles was that narrator. Julie Haydon underplayed the part of the modern Borgia almost to the point of vocal extinction, while Bob Emery and Ted Osborne each put plenty of dread into their lines. The scoring of the musical bridges was of standout quality.   Odec.

144

conflicting. Unfortunately, there are only two programs from this short season, the first and the last: *Burning Court* and *Cave of Ali Baba*. All of the rest are mysteries as to whether or not they aired, and if so, exactly when they did!

The most common collector listing of that summer's programs is as follows:

06/17/42 The Burning Court
06/24/42 Wet Saturday
07/01/42 The Life of Nellie James
07/08/42 Rope
07/15/42 The Third Eye
07/22/42 Witness on the Westbound Ltd
07/29/42 Philomel Cottage
08/05/42 Finishing School
08/12/42 Suspicion
08/19/42 The Cave of Ali Baba

These listings were likely created by referencing newspaper archives as well as scripts, when available.

Producer William Spier's papers reside at the University of Wisconsin of Wisconsin and can be accessed there. There are copies of certain scripts in the collection. The library's website lists some script information.

http://digicoll.library.wisc.edu/cgi/f/findaid/findaid-idx?c=wiarchives;cc=wiarchives;q1=william%20spier;rgn=main;view=text;didno=uw-whs-us0097an

What's surprising is that the collection even has copies of scripts for programs that he was not assigned to. That's very helpful. A listing of the Spier holdings indicates the following:

06/17/42 NO SCRIPT AVAILABLE
06/24/42 Wet Saturday
07/01/42 The Life of Nellie James
07/08/42 Rope
07/15/42 Witness on the Westbound Limited
07/22/42 NO SCRIPT AVAILABLE
07/29/42 Philomel Cottage
08/05/42 NO SCRIPT AVAILABLE
08/12/42 Suspicion
08/19/42 The Cave of Ali Baba

Note that there is no copy of *The Burning Court*, but that's not a problem because there are other sources of information, including the recording, that make it quite clear it was the first program. There are other differences, and it should be stressed that Spier's papers were likely not available to the creators of the original log. These are the differences:

- The log lists *The Third Eye* as the program for 1942-07-15, while Spier's papers do not have a program of that title and instead have *Witness on the Westbound Limited* in that date instead. Below is a listing of the web page image.

Box 17   "The Witness on the West-Bound Limited," 1942 July 15
Folder 7   **Note**
                  Prod: Charles Vanda

                  Dir: Charles Vanda

                  Script: Harold Medford

- There is no script for 1942-08-05 in the collection.

Spier's papers should be considered as authoritative. Further research by collector Don Ramlow implies that these are scripts that were prior to production, so there were cast changes and other edits that were made later. Mr. Ramlow has had access to copies of many of Harold Medford's scripts from this season with further markups.

It was originally thought that *The Third Eye* was an adaptation of the Robert Chambers book of that name published in the early 1900s. Chambers wrote the original *Mr. Keen, Tracer of Lost Persons* novel.

Research by Mr. Ramlow and verified by myself and collector Keith Scott has indicated that *The Third Eye is* a novel by Ethel Lina White. Some may be familiar with the name because she

 wrote *The Lady Vanishes* which was adapted into a famous early Alfred Hitchcock movie. Details about the *Third Eye* novel are at http://inkquilletc.blogspot.com/2017/03/forgott en-book-third-eye-by-ethel-lina.html

The name was changed by the *Suspense* producers to *Finishing School*. This means that there was no *Third Eye* broadcast. What was thought to be a missing show was never missing at all. It was just performed with a different title.

This next table represents the latest thinking (at least by this author) of the 1942 summer for *Suspense*. The items in **bold** are believed to be indisputable at this time. The other dates are still requiring research and a bit of luck.

06/17/42 **The Burning Court**
06/24/42 **Wet Saturday**
07/01/42 **The Life of Nellie James**
07/08/42 **Rope**
07/15/42 **Witness on the Westbound Ltd**
07/22/42 Finishing School
07/29/42 **Philomel Cottage**
08/05/42 NO SCRIPT ????
08/12/42 Suspicion
08/19/42 **The Cave of Ali Baba**

After *The Cave of Ali Baba, Suspense* was pre-empted on 1942-08-26 for a special program about the release of the movie *Holiday Inn*.

The following week, 1942-09-02, was a performance of Lucille Fletcher's *The Hitch-hiker* starring Orson Welles. The program had been performed in 1941 on Lady Esther Screen Guild; a recording does not exist.

Suspense was pre-empted the following week for war news and commentary. Then, starting on 1942-09-16, *Suspense* began its full-fledged broadcast life with most every broadcast preserved and documented in some way.

In many ways, that summer of 1942 remains a mystery.
Mr. Ramlow has the best chance of unraveling it all through his continuing and diligent research.

Fury and Sound, A Most Curious Missing Episode of *Suspense*

This is a remarkably curious episode written by some important radio professionals. The story is about a mad narcissist producer who terrorizes his staff and performers in the studio. We know what this episode is like because a short story version of it was featured in the first issue of *Suspense Magazine.*

The script is an over-the-top performance with deliberate overacting. One can see this, literally, in the television production of it on *The Unexpected* which has Hans Conried in the starring role. It's such a strange script, that one has to wonder if it was held for summer broadcast when fewer people would be listening.

Why would such high-powered radio luminaries write such a farcical script? Because they they mentored William Spier in his early radio work, and they were pleased with his success. This is, in effect, a "roast" of Spier, and his reputation, in which he was a willing participant.

Scriptwriters **Jerome Lawrence and Robert E. Lee** were part of the group who founded AFRS and helped develop exclusive programming like *Command Performance* and *Mail Call.* The collaborators had successful careers in theater and television. They wrote the play *Inherit the Wind* (1955). More details about their work is at http://archives.nypl.org/the/21482.

Irving Reis was a pivotal figure in the development of radio production, founding the experimental series *Columbia*

Workshop. He left radio for Hollywood as a writer and director

of films in the *Falcon* series and the movie *The Bachelor and the Bobby-Soxer*. He died at age 47, a year after the *Unexpected* version first aired. https://en.wikipedia.org/wiki/Irving_Reis His last radio play was *Man from Tomorrow*, broadcast on *Suspense* on 1957-09-01.

This was also quite an unusual script for *Suspense*. "Mark Humboldt" is listed in the cast and in the press materials --- *but he does not exist!* (And just to verify, I checked that there are no records of such a person in IMDb or at Playbill.com or newspapers.com, *Billboard*, or *Variety*). Another actor, "Clifton Cromwell" is listed in the cast, too, *and doesn't exist either!*

Lawrence, Lee, and Reis, all worked with Spier early in their careers. Spier was known as a prodigy of early radio, and his fellow professionals respected his rise… and his sense of humor. Spier was known to be a demanding executive, but he would often keep the rehearsals and other meetings "light."

According to collector Keith Scott, the name "Mark Humboldt" was used in *Sam Spade* (which Spier produced). When Sam would tell people to use a name as part of some kind of deception (such as in the 9/12/48 *The Lazarus Caper*) or Spade would use that name himself as an alias (as in 12/14/47 *The Gumshoe Caper*, 12/21/47 *The Nick Saint Caper*). These examples were well after the 1945 broadcast of *Fury and Sound* but may have been used at other times in the *Spade* series. Of these *Spade* episodes, only *The Lazarus Caper* exists.

Humboldt and Cromwell? The names could have been joke names that were always used when levity was required or they just needed a name, much like "John Doe" or "John Q. Public" are used. They are likely derived from names of towns in Connecticut near where producer William Spier had property and had lived.

The joke about "Mark Humboldt" is even bigger. It was included in the press releases CBS sent to newspapers about the episode. What makes this even stranger was that a publicity photographer was staging pictures at the rehearsals for this particular episode.

 Pictures can be seen at
https://www.gettyimages.com/photos/suspense-fury-and-sound-lloyd?phrase=suspense%20%22fury%20and%20sound%22%20lloyd#license

The star of the episode is Norman Lloyd (who, as of this writing, is 103 yrs old and still with us), supported by radio great Lurene Tuttle. The picture on the Getty site (not included in the book because of copyright reasons) also includes Spier, and two production professionals... but no "Humboldt" (supposedly the co-star!) or "Cromwell."

The surviving script of the program was not used in production and does not include the rehearsal revisions or the names of the actors assigned to "be" Humboldt or Cromwell.

At the end of the program, Spier comes to the microphone! He refers to himself as "Spier" just like the character in the story refers to himself in the third person by last name only. He says that he hopes everyone "enjoyed the little expose of backstage radio." He thanks the cast, mixing the names of Humboldt and Cromwell in with those of the real actors Norman Lloyd and

Lurene Tuttle, and then the production staff.

He says "tonight's story was all in the spirit of fun and was completely fictional. There are no such characters among us producers as Kingsley Roeschler..." After a few more words, he calls out to Bill Johnstone, not by name, and says "and *you...* when you say *Suspense* is produced, edited, and directed by William Spier, I want a great deal more importance there... those are the most vital words in the show." Johnstone dutifully agrees and then proceeds to close the show as normal.

```
MR. SPIER:   This is William Spier.  Spier wants you to know that
             he hopes you have enjoyed tonight's little expose
             of backstage radio.  I want to thank all our cast....
             Norman Lloyd, Mark Humboldt, Miss Lurene Tuttle,
             Clifton Cromwell _____. And thanks
             as always to Lud Gluskin, our conductor, Lucian Moraweck
             for his score, Berne Surrey for sound effects, and
             Ted Denton, our engineer.  I should like you to know,
             of course, that tonight's story was all in the spirit
             of fun, and was completely fictional.  There are no
             such characters among us producers as Kingsley Roeschler
             and any resemblance to actual persons etc.  .....So
             Spier says Goodnight...oh...and you....

NARR:        Me? Yes, sir.

SPIER:       When you say Suspense is produced, edited, and
             directed by William Spier...I want a great deal more
             importance there.  Those are the most vital words in the
             show.

NARR:        Yes, sir.  Next Thursday, same time, Joan Lorring we
             will be your star of (KNIFE CHORD) SUSPENSE.
```

Perhaps one day the recording this very different program will be shared among collectors. But until then, we will have to rely on the script and other information we can gather, and the production of the short story performed by *Blue Hours Productions* (a link is in the chapter about missing episodes).

Mysterious Authors: Who are They?

There are some interesting stories about some of the authors and pseudonyms of some *Suspense* episodes.

On a Country Road *by Walter Bazar*

This is the popular episode about a couple trapped in their disabled car during a heavy storm while police seek a deranged killer. Its author was Walter Bazar, a Columbia University journalism student, whose work was never heard on radio again. The episode was repeated a few times, and was even used on the *Suspense* television series. Bazar went on to have a good career, working mainly for the *New York Journal-American* as a reporter, usually specializing in science-and government-related news.

Tree of Life *by J. Douglas Ware*

This is a sad but heartwarming story about a sister memorializing her brother who died in WW2 combat. No, that's not the plot of the script, that's the backstory of the author. Joan Ware worked at CBS in a variety of positions. She wrote this story when she was a clerk in the script department. Joan and her brother conceived it prior to the war. He served in the Air Force in Europe and was killed in combat. Joan completed the script and it was accepted for *Suspense*. She wanted no credit, just her brother's name as author as a memorial to him. Another script, *Backlash*, was used on *The Whistler*. These are the only scripts written by "J. Douglas Ware" that are known. Joan continued to work at CBS, and further research indicates she later left the company to work at a Hollywood public relations firm.

Four Episodes: Mission of the Betta, Steel River Prison Break, Treasure Chest of Don Jose, *and* The Wreck Of The Old 97, *by Christopher Anthony*

There are some who attribute scripts by Christopher Anthony to one of radio's geniuses, Antony Ellis, but we now know that is incorrect. It was a different radio genius: William N. Robson. These four *Suspense* episodes and two *Romance* episodes, *This Above All*, and *Return To Tomorrow*, were written by "Christopher Anthony." There may be others yet to be documented.

Why? Christopher and Anthony were the names of Robson's first two sons. Robson was likely "hiding" his identity because he was producing the *Modern Adventures of Casanova* starring Errol Flynn (not a very good show) over at the Mutual network at that time while also ducking some unnecessary attention in the *Red Channels* scare that seemed to preoccupy some individual CBS executives.

Future broadcasts of *Treasure Chest of Don Jose* and *Steel River Prison Break* mentioned Robson as the author on the script documents and as part of the on-air announcements. These clips are from the three *Treasure Chest of Don Jose* scripts.

May 4, 1952	Gluskin. "The Treasure Chest of Don Jose" was written for Suspense by Christopher Anthony. Featured in the
June 26, 1956	AUTHOR: WILLIAM N. ROBSON
October 11, 1958	"The Treasure Chest of Don Jose" by William N. Robson

Many episodes by Jonathan Bundy

Yours Truly, Johnny Dollar fans will recognize this name as a pseudonym of Jack Johnstone. He had a long radio career in a variety of positions but is best known as the superb writer, director, and producer of *YTJD*. His tenure began with the highly regarded 5-part serials in 1955 through the end of the Hollywood production at the end of summer 1959. Johnstone kept writing for the series after it moved to New York until it ended in September 1962. Johnstone's contribution to *Suspense* was for the 1962 episodes *Feathers*, *Friday*, *The Curse of Kamashek* (adapted from the *YTJD* serial), *Formula for Death*, and the final *Suspense* broadcast, *Devilstone*. His career is fascinating, and more can be learned in John C. Abbott's *YTJD* books.

Sorry, Wrong Number: The Famous *Suspense* Episode that Spanned the Media and the Generations

Sorry, Wrong Number was the legendary *Suspense* broadcast written by Lucille Fletcher that became a famous movie, a record album, numerous television presentations, a theatrical play, and even an opera! It was performed on *Suspense* multiple times, and is still being performed today by theater groups and by fans presenting recreations.

This following pages are not intended to be a detailed exposition about the episode, but a collection of curiosities. Some myths are debunked, but the more you dig into this famous radio play, the more awe you have for it.

For simplicity, the abbreviation *SWN* is used in some parts of this section.

First, the Title

Collectors and researchers Keith Scott and Don Ramlow have done extensive research about the series. It is known for certain that William Spier created the title. Lucille Fletcher, the author, seemed to better at compelling stories than the titles they should have. According to Keith's research, the first title was *I'm So Nervous*. Then, it seems to have changed to *She Overheard Death Talking* which was included in press releases, but *She Overheard Murder Speaking* was announced in prior week's show. Don Ramlow found a production script with the title *If at First You Don't Succeed*! That was crossed out, with the title *Sorry, Wrong Number* replacing it. Spier certainly created a winning title.

Liner notes for the *SWN* Decca record set mention the title *You Can Always Telephone*. Spier's selection was so much better.

The Basics

The plotline is this: A wealthy, neurotic, bed-ridden woman is alone at home. Her only contact with the world is her phone. One night, because of a "crossed wire" on the phone lines, she hears another conversation, which are plans for a murder in her neighborhood on the Upper East Side of Manhattan timed for the noise of a passing train as cover for the killer's actions. She frantically calls others who might be able to stop the murder, including the phone operator. She explains what she heard, and is distressed by their lack of urgency and cooperation. As the drama continues, she realizes she is the murderer's target. We never fully hear the killing with the subway noise increasing in volume, as was planned so nefariously. Her screams are heard in the background, and as the train passes in the distance and its noise subsides, we hear the thud of her body falling to the floor. This made the story quite different for radio dramas of the time, when most stories ended with villains being thwarted.

The show seems dated today, because land line phones are much less common, replaced by mobile technologies. At the time of the broadcast, however, fewer than 40% of US households had phones, because they were either too expensive for families or considered an unnecessary luxury. This made the story all the more interesting and curious to the public because so many aspired to own a home phone! Social class envy may have been a factor in the show's horror. Nowadays the idea of "dialing" a phone that is outdated, even though it is used in daily language.

SWN put *Suspense* into the spotlight. Though there was a flubbed line at the end of its initial performance, no one had heard such a radio play before, where the subject is killed and there is no attempt to save them. The emotional and tension-building performance of Agnes Moorehead was a first for many listeners. Already known as a superb actress, this became her defining role. Aspiring actors would study her performance many years after the original broadcast.

Suspense still did not have a sponsor when *SWN* was first broadcast. It is likely that the performance began to set the series apart from other dramas in listener minds, but especially in the way CBS approached potential advertisers. The "word of mouth" discussion of the story among listeners after the first broadcast was quite strong. There were many letters received (and phone calls, of course!) by CBS and its stations asking to explain the ending.

The Famous Mistake

The performance was so intense that an important line uttered by the killer ("Oh, police department...") was delivered at the wrong time (before the police officer calling could say "Police department, Sergeant Martin speaking."). It is not known if this was a missed cue by an actor or a mistake by the director in giving the wrong cue.

The following week's program, *Banquo's Chair*, began with an announcement that *SWN* would be presented again because of popular demand to understand the play's proper ending.

One of the beneficial effects of the error may have been its effect on future *Suspense* performances. They are usually virtually flawless; even separate recordings of east and west coast performances can be played simultaneously have just microseconds of timing differences. The *SWN* incident may have instilled an obsession with precision that other programs did not have. This is another reason to hold it in high regard.

SWN, *The Legend*

The episode developed quite a following, and listeners enjoyed hearing it again and again. The reputation lasted for decades, especially with the success of the movie which brought it to new audiences.

SWN was entered into the National Recording Registry in 2015. At that website, an interesting item is presented that provides insight into Fletcher's inspiration:

> ...in "Sorry, Wrong Number," Stevenson's "only crime was being a not very kind person," says Dorothy Herrmann, Lucille Fletcher's daughter. Herrmann sees the play as her mother's way of getting back at the stuck-up mother of her college boyfriend. "She looked down on my mother," who was a "scholarship student," Herrmann says. "This made my mother very miserable." The moral of Fletcher's tale? Be nice.

This is just part of a brief interview with Dorothy Herrmann; the interview can be accessed at the Registry site.
https://beta.prx.org/stories/166087

There's yet another story, also reported by daughter Dorothy, which was part of the *New York Times* obituary for Fletcher on June 6, 2000:

Her daughter Dorothy Herrmann said Miss Fletcher got the idea for the drama after an obnoxious well-dressed woman refused to permit her to go ahead on a supermarket checkout line on Manhattan's East Side when Miss Fletcher was buying some milk or cereal for one of her children, who was sick.

"No, you cannot," the woman said. "How dare you?"

The drama, Ms. Herrmann said, was Miss Fletcher's act of revenge.

Which story was correct? There are enough annoying people in the world that Fletcher probably made the lead *SWN* character a composite of the ones she disliked most.

Agnes Moorehead Tried to Buy the Script

Sorry, Wrong Number was such a lucrative property for Agnes Moorehead that she tried to buy it in 1947, according to columnist Hedda Hopper. Lucille Fletcher turned the offer down. It was sold to the producer of the 1948 movie, Anatole Litvak. Producer Billy Wilder tried to buy it from Litvak for $150,000; that's $1.7 million in today's dollars, and Litvak refused. This may have been Moorehead trying to ensure she would get the lead role in the movie. That went to Barbara Stanwyck, instead. Moorehead knew, however, that there would be future opportunities for *SWN* on radio, television, the stage, and recordings such as the Decca radio release, in North America and abroad. Despite not starring in the movie, she made the best of those opportunities she still had.

The tag lines for the movie are interesting, especially two of the six used:

- *She overheard the plans for her own destruction!*
  (sounds like a derivative of one of the working titles

used when the radio performance was being prepared)

- *The prize-winning radio suspense drama that thrilled 40,000,000 people ... now electrifies the screen!* (this indicates the magnitude of how *SWN* changed the public perception of the *Suspense* radio series; the US population was 136 million at the time)

Was There a Corrected and Error-Free West Coast Performance of SWN on May 25, 1943?

It has often been believed among collectors, perhaps for more than 40 years, that there was a separate west coast error-free performance of *SWN*. In the early years of collecting on reels and cassettes, there were recordings identified as the mistakeless west coast version of *Sorry, Wrong Number.*

Newspaper radio timetables show there was no west coast broadcast. At this time in the program's history, *Suspense* was performed *once* for the entire CBS network, heard on the east coast at 9:30pm, and through the times zones at that equivalent moment. West coast listeners heard the show at 6:30pm. It was not until Roma Wines began its sponsorship later that year that there were east and west coast performances, and those weren't even on the same day!

The clips also included some of the other titles for the show. Press releases had already been sent out with the title *She Overheard Death Speaking.*

This is the *New York Times* listing, for 9:30pm Eastern Time:

Play: "She Overheard Death Speaking." With Agnes Moorehead. Others —WABC, 9:30-10.

The *Wisconsin State Journal* lists the program for 8:30pm Central Time

> ⁞ ᴊ ᴜᴄᴇ ᴛᴛᴏᴀᴊᴠᴇᴄ ᴠᴀᴛᴀᴛ.ᴇᴠ.
>
> 8:30 p. m. — Suspense (WCCO):
> Agnes Moorehead in "She Over-
> heard Death Speaking."

The *Salt Lake Tribune* lists *Suspense* in the Mountain Time Zone for 7:30pm

> **7:30** ★Spotlight Bands ...... ⊙Suspense ......
> **7:45** ★7:55—News ....

California's *Long Beach Independent* lists the program at 6:30pm Pacific Time....

> "SHE OVERHEARD DEATH SPEAKING," written by Lu-cile Fletcher and starring Agnes Moorehead, will provide a thrilling half-hour for KNX "Suspense" listeners tonight at 6:30. Producer William Spier explains that in the broadcast Miss Moorehead's voice will be the only one heard except unidentified voices on the the telephone. The climax of the story should jar "Suspense" listeners to their heels.

as does the *Los Angeles Times*...

> **6:30 P.M.**
> KFWB—Strollin' Tom.
> KMPC—'Thru' the Years.
> KMTR—Bill of Rights.
> KOPJ—American-Jewish Hr.
> KPAS—Aircraft News.
> KFI—Fibber McGee, Molly.
> KNX—Suspense.
> KHJ—Return Nick Carter.
> KFVD—Roundup.
> KECA—Spotlight Bands.
> KGER—Music.

The show would be repeated on August 21, as noted in the *Decatur Herald* of that date.

> Columbia network's "Suspense" series changes to a new day and time today, when it will be heard on WSOY at 6:30 o'clock. The mystery series will continue to be heard hereafter on Saturdays. Tonight's play wil' be "Sorry, Wrong Number." starring Agnes Moorehead. The play is being repeated by popular request.

Note that there's *no mention of the missed cue*... just that the program is repeated because of "popular request." The show was repeated because the audience was confused... and because the show's producers realized they had a script and performance that engaged the radio audience in a manner that previous episodes had not.

And what of those purported "west coast" recordings of a corrected performance? Those recordings were either created by editing the miscue out or by inserting the correct section of dialogue from a later performance.

There are many old recordings that were "repaired" in an effort to restore problem programs. In the 1960s and 1970s collectors believed that they were part of a major grass roots effort to save old radio recordings and preserve the history of the era.

However the purported west coast recording was created, it was incorrect, even if it was done with the best intentions to preserve OTR history.

How Many Times was SWN *Broadcast?*

SWN was performed many times and on different continents. It is probably impossible to count them exactly, but these are the most important ones.

US productions

- *Suspense* 1943-05-25 Agnes Moorehead
- *Suspense* 1943-08-21 Agnes Moorehead
- *Suspense* 1944-02-24 Agnes Moorehead (Roma Wines Thursday East Coast performance) (missing)
- *Suspense* 1944-02-28 Agnes Moorehead (Roma Wines Monday West Coast performance)
- *Kate Smith Show* 1945-05-20 Ida Lupino (abridged sketch) (missing)
- *Suspense* 1945-09-06 Agnes Moorehead
- *Radio Hall of Fame* 1946-03-24 Agnes Moorehead (abridged sketch)
- *Suspense* 1948-11-18 Agnes Moorehead
- *Suspense* 1952-09-15 Agnes Moorehead (missing)
- *Suspense* 1957-10-20 Agnes Moorehead
- *Suspense* 1960-02-14 Agnes Moorehead (was a replay of the 1957 taped performance with the 1960 format *Suspense* opening and closing announcements edited in).

BBC Productions

- BBC Light Programme 1948-12-31 Flora Robson
- BBC Light Programme 1949-03-15 Flora Robson
- BBC Home Service 1956-06-01 Nottingham Playhouse Company

Movie adaptation back to radio

- *Lux Radio Theatre* (US) 1950-01-09 Barbara Stanwyck

- *Lux Radio Theatre* (Australia) 1955-02-20 Miriam Hopkins; this visit by Ms. Hopkins was covered for weeks in Australia's press. At that time, flying from San Francisco to Sydney was more than 30 hours with three fuel stops. Hopkins' visit was intended to get publicity for the new season of *Lux* but also to interest more travel to Australia and to entice more Hollywood actors to appear in their programs.

How Many Times Did Moorehead Step Before the Microphone?

SWN was performed many times by Moorehead, and not always for *Suspense.*

- 1) 1943-05-23 performed once
- 2) 1943-08-21 performed once
- 3) 1944-02-24 Roma Wines Thursday east coast
- 4) 1944-02-28 Roma Wines Monday west coast
- 5 & 6) 1945-09-06 it is likely there were two performances, one for the east and one for the west a few hours later
- *7 & 8) 1946-03-24 Radio Hall of Fame* likely performed twice for east and west coast audiences in an abridged performance
- 9) 1947 recording for Decca Records
- 10 & 11) 1948-11-18 likely east and west coast
- 12) 1952-09-15 likely performed once for transcribed broadcast for time zones was more common
- 13) 1957-10-20 performed once for taped broadcast

That is 13 different times in live or recorded performances for new broadcasts. The 1960-02-14 *Suspense* was an edited version of the 1957 performance and does not count toward the total. Newspaper press releases, however, were written to imply that it was a new performance in an attempt to draw listeners.

The *Radio Hall of Fame* performance is interesting in light of Moorehead's comments to the press about the occasion. The 1946-09-16 *Cincinnati OH Enquirer* reported that the performance before a live audience was "a terrifically nerve-wracking experience."

She explained:

> I have to work myself up to such a hysterical pitch for the part that distractions of any kind could ruin the entire effect. People in a studio audience, absorbed and tense, are apt to get a little hysterical, to laugh at the wrong time, squeal at a sound effect or do something else to destroy the mood or break the spell.

Her next comment was on behalf of the listening audience.

> Since such outbursts have to go unexplained, it is unfair to the listeners, too... I am convinced that studio audiences would be better banned at all dramatic shows.

Suspense had a strict no-audience rule, which a 1945 news item in *Tune In* magazine stated was an attraction for many movie actors because it was like being on the closed movie sets they were used to.

The missing 1952 Sorry, Wrong Number *broadcast: an insight into* Suspense *history*

Thanks to the research efforts of Suspense researcher Don Ramlow, we have access to a copy of the script for the 1952 performance. A recording of the episode is unfortunately missing. The script cover page alone is a window into how production technology and methods had changed from just a few years before.

The upper left hand corner identifies the script as the Monday, September 15, 1952 program and that dramatic portions were recorded separately on Friday, September 5, 1952, ten days earlier.

The lower right hand corner shows the cast appearing for read-through and rehearsals at 1:00pm on September 5. All times are US Pacific time zone. The final recording of the dramatic portions was from 5:30 to 6:00pm.

The orchestra and commercial staff (announcers) came for rehearsals on September 15 beginning at 2:00pm, with their performances, combined with the playing of the transcription, aired live beginning at 5:00pm Pacific time to the network. Pacific listeners did not get it until 9:00pm that night, when a fully transcribed program with combined drama, music, and commercials, was played.

The lower left corner shows the dates for production staff to report. Those persons with no dates next to their names were to appear on both days.

It is interesting that the dramatic portion of the program was directed by William Spier, even though this was the Elliott Lewis era of Suspense. From the beginning of the *SWN* legacy, there was a close professional association of Moorehead, Spier, and author Lucille Fletcher that also included the Decca Record release and another popular *Suspense* script, *Diary of Sophronia Winters*.

The 1952 production was the first of the new season of *Suspense*, and was used as a public relations event. The TV-Radio editor of the *Los Angeles Times*, Walter Ames, described the recording session of September 5 in his column of September 15. He details the command presence of William Spier, *Suspense's* legendary producer-director just for the event and that "the cast probably constituted one of the highest priced supporting groups ever gathered for a mystery show."

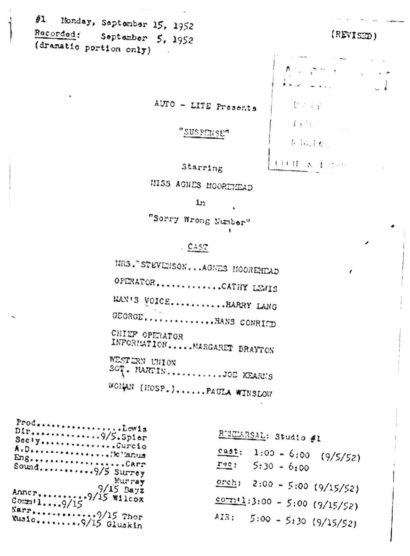

#1   Monday, September 15, 1952
Recorded: September 5, 1952   (REVISED)
(dramatic portion only)

AUTO - LITE Presents

"SUSPENSE"

Starring

MISS AGNES MOOREHEAD

in

"Sorry Wrong Number"

CAST

MRS. STEVENSON...AGNES MOOREHEAD

OPERATOR.............CATHY LEWIS

MAN'S VOICE..........HARRY LANG

GEORGE..............HANS CONRIED

CHIEF OPERATOR
INFORMATION.....MARGARET BRAYTON

WESTERN UNION
SGT. MARTIN..........JOE KEARNS

WOMAN (HOSP.)......PAULA WINSLOW

Prod..................Lewis
Dir.............9/5.Spier
Secty..............Curcio
A.D................McManus
Eng...................Carr
Sound.........9/5 Surrey
                    Murray
Anncr..........9/15 Bayz
Comm'l....9/15 9/15 Wilcox
Narr..........9/15
Music........9/15 Gluskin

REHEARSAL: Studio #1

cast: 1:00 - 6:00 (9/5/52)
rec: 5:30 - 6:00

orch: 2:00 - 5:00 (9/15/52)
comm'l:3:00 - 5:00 (9/15/52)
AIR: 5:00 - 5:30 (9/15/52)

Ames writes that viewing the preparations to record the performance was "like watching a football coach briefing his team in the locker room before kickoff." He noted that Elliott Lewis stepped aside for the day, as Spier and Moorehead had done *SWN* so many times before. Because this was just the recording of the drama, Lewis would still be the producer and director when the show aired with live orchestra and the announcers as the transcription played.In his article, Ames makes a technical "error" that is insightful to us, almost 70 years later. He says, at its end, that "it would have been easier to have replayed one of the old tape recordings."

It's a casual jargon error. We're sure Ames knew that radio programs were recorded on transcription discs and that tape did not enter the production scene until after WW2.

Suspense was late in adopting full recording tape production methods, not doing so until Fall 1956 when William N. Robson took over the program. Ames' comment is more an indication about how recording tape had so strongly started its adoption that "tape" quickly entered the industry vocabulary and referred to any kind archived recording, at least in his mind and that of his readers.

SWN was a beloved episode, even though the script had a gruesome conclusion. In 1952 there were still many *Suspense* listeners who had never heard it performed. It was four years since the most recent broadcast of it.

The year 1952 was one of a few years of turbulent media change and growth. Listening patterns had been altered by the broadening presence of television. Even though the radio audience was diminishing, when one factors in the amount of time that had passed since the last *SWN* broadcast, the presence of new listeners among the established fans guaranteed a much different audience.

It was easy for Ames, who tracked TV and radio every single

day, to momentarily lose that perspective. It's not a repeat if you never heard it before.

As mentioned earlier, this performance of *SWN* was originally scheduled for June 1952. It was delayed to become the first broadcast of the Fall 1952 season, replaced in the June slot by *Concerto for Killer and Eyewitnesses.*

Don't lose that number... the many phone numbers of SWN

Phone numbers used to have named exchanges that identified sections of town. In this case it was "Murray Hill," or MU (the numbers 6 and 8). Murray Hill was a generally upper middle and upper class section of Manhattan. Today, the generic exchange of 555 is used in numbers because so many listeners or viewers would call the numbers to see who answered or what happened, resulting in many nuisance calls for customers. 555 is a permanently reserved exchange for phone company use only.

MU 7-0093	1943 and 1952 performances
MU 4-0098	1944 and 1945 performances, *Radio Hall of Fame*, and Decca Records
MU 4-0599	1948 and 1957 performances

First Television Performance

SWN was performed on television a few times. It was an early offering, presented live, to a very small audience of what was still an experimental medium for broadcasters and their advertisers. It aired on the CBS New York channel on January 30, 1946 and starred

Mildred Natwick. The cast is detailed at IMDb. https://www.imdb.com/title/tt0311839/fullcredits?ref_=tt_cl_sm#cast

The performance did not get good reviews. It was done on the CBS-TV network and was produced by famed actor John Housman. He was part of Orson Welles' Mercury Theater, as was Agnes Moorehead. Natwick was selected because Moorehead was in California, and could not be in New York at that time. Remember, even by air travel, which was not very pleasant at that time because they flew at lower altitudes compared to today where there was more turbulence, cross-country flights had to stop two or three times to refuel, and would take almost a day, aside from being expensive.

There is a picture of Natwick in the role at the Getty Images site. https://www.gettyimages.com/photos/natwick-sorry-wrong-number?phrase=natwick%20sorry%20wrong%20number#license

The director of the program was Frances Buss, one of television broadcasting's first woman executives. An interview of Buss, where she briefly mentions the program, can be found at https://interviews.televisionacademy.com/interviews/frances-buss-buch

Mildred Natwick appeared on *Suspense* once in 1945 for *The Furnished Floor*, which was also written by Fletcher. She was on the TV version of *Suspense* in 1951 in an adaptation of another radio episode held in high regard, *On a Country Road*.

Decca Records

SWN was so popular that Decca Records was able to market a recording of it. This was not an edited version of one of the radio broadcasts. This was a new production.

The post-WW2 boom in consumer spending led many households to purchase record players, not just televisions. It was believed that the "spoken word" category of releases would be of interest to a great many consumers. *SWN* was an obvious choice to be made available in this way. The first set was released in 1947 on 78s, an LP version appears to be released around 1952, with another around 1958. The initial release was a great success.

Decca set, 1947, on 78s

Label from the 1947 release

Decca set, 1952, LP edition

It was so successful that radio stations that were not CBS affiliates or did not broadcast *Suspense* started playing the record set on the air! *Radio Daily* reported in November 1948 that Moorehead was taking legal action against disc jockeys to stop them. *Radio Mirror* reported the same thing a few months later.

Despite the success of the *SWN* recordings, no great parade of other favorite radio episodes appearing in record stores. *SWN* was one of the few radio programs that could be financially viable in such a small niche market that became dominated by news recordings such as Edward R. Murrow's records *Hear It Now* and recordings of theatrical stage plays.

There is a copy of the Decca recording from the 1947 set on YouTube https://www.youtube.com/watch?v=vGqdp89tDfY

Sorry, Wrong Number: *The Opera?*

Yes, not just one, but two operas! These were short performances, and usually performed at opera festivals.

The first was by Lucille Fletcher, written in the late 1970s with composer Jerome Moross. He became a close friend while she was married to composer Bernard Herrmann. This is a description of a 1982 performance from the *New York Times*:

> Jerome Moross's "Sorry, Wrong Number" also had a focused subject and tone, but its overlong libretto by Lucille Fletcher and Mr. Moross's single-minded cinematic suspense music made Stephanie Low earnestly strain at her vocal lines; the final murder was a bit of a relief.

Low was an accomplished opera singer of the time.

That comment "the final murder was a bit of a relief" is the way a lot of people feel after listening to *SWN*, not just the opera. Honestly, that's part of the craft of Fletcher's work. Listeners become impatient with Mrs. Stevenson's antics in the story. That conflicted feeling is intensified when the show ends with her murder, and the listener realizing that they were voyeurs to a gruesome crime. This is why the story has such great disturbing personal and guilt-inducing effect on the listener.

As a radio play, it works and is why the play was so memorable. As an opera, it gets tedious, and does not create that chilling effect.

Sadly, this was Moross' final work after decades of success composing for ballet, theater, motion pictures, and original classical works.

As if that wasn't warning enough, another respected composer tried it again. Jack Beeson had written ten operas in his career and taught music at Columbia University.

The recording of the opera is for sale at https://www.albanyrecords.com/mm5/merchant.mvc?Screen=PROD&Store_Code=AR&Product_Code=TROY1009&Category_Code=a-NR

A recording of the opera by Beeson is also up at YouTube https://www.youtube.com/watch?v=uJVA6qv5KH0

Episodic Curiosities
Thank Goodness Someone Changed the Title!

Final broadcast titles and their pre-broadcast working titles were not always the same. It is likely that there are more; these were found from newspaper listings and scripts we had access to. Authors may have changed titles many times on their own prior to submission.

BROADCAST TITLE	WORKING TITLE(S)
2462	2461
A Killing in Abilene	Innocent in Abilene
Angel of Death	Before the Fact
Banquo's Chair	The Extra Guest
Big Shot	Break-Up
Blackjack to Kill	Assassin
Bon Voyage	End of the Line
Consequence	Revenge
The Day I Died	Revenge
Finishing School	The Third Eye
Firing Run	Firing Gun
Freedom this Way	Flight to the West
House in Cypress Canyon	House in Cypress Gardens
I Had an Alibi	Murder is Simple
The Lady in the Red Hat	The Thirteenth Apostle
Love and Times of Joaquin Murietta	California Outlaw; Joaquin Murietta, California Outlaw
The Marvelous Barastro	The Human Barastro
McKay College Basketball Scandal	The Losing Game of Frederick Hudson

BROADCAST TITLE	WORKING TITLE(S)
Murder and Aunt Delia	Murder of My Aunt
Murder of Necessity	The Frame-Up; Backfire
Murderous Revision; Murder on Mike	The Twist is Death; The Twist is Murder; The Twisted Murder
The Mutiny of the Marie Celeste	The Case of the Mutiny of the Marie Celeste
Perchance to Dream	To Sleep, Perchance to Dream
Pretty Girl	Baby Sitter
The Rose Garden	Miss Bone
Sorry, Wrong Number	You Can Always Telephone; I'm So Nervous; She Overheard Death Talking; She Overheard Murder Speaking; If at First You Don't Succeed
The Sure Thing	The Fix
The Thirteenth Sound	Dying is Safer
To Find Help	The Man
Treasure Chest of Don Jose	Treasure Hunt
Two Platinum Capsules	Two Platinum Needles
The Victoria Cross	The Housemaster
Vidocq's Final Case	Vidocq

Some of these different titles appeared in newspaper clippings, as noted earlier. Press releases were mailed weeks before the show was broadcast, and a lot could happen in that lag of time.

There were other situations where the working title was announced on air in the previous week's broadcast and was changed just days before the live performance.

The broadcast title was the final choice of the producer, and authors may not have been consulted. In many cases, it's a good thing they were changed!

Sound Familiar? Same Script, Different Name

Suspense re-used scripts now and then, especially years after the original broadcast, when an episode was likely to reach a different audience. Or, perhaps it was just believed to be a better title the second time around for a script that deserved repeating. In some cases, this is good news, because that repeat performance turned out to be one of a missing episode.

TITLE USED IN FIRST BROADCAST	REPEAT TITLE
Butcher's Wife	Never Steal a Butcher's Wife
Case Study of a Murderer	Study of a Murderer
Escape of Lacey Abbott	Mad Man of Manhattan
Eve	The Black Angel
Fresh Air, Sunshine, and Murder (missing episode)	Rub Down and Out
Hitch-hike Poker	Four of a Kind
Jack Ketch	Groom of the Ladder
Mr. Markham, Antique Dealer	Dealings of Mr. Markham
Misfortune in Pearls (missing episode)	End of the String
Murderous Revision	Murder on Mike
Neal Cream, Doctor of Poison	A Study of Poison
Nobody Ever Quits	Night on Red Mountain
Tale of Two Sisters	The Ten Years
Three Times Murder	Murder Strikes Three Times

TITLE USED IN FIRST BROADCAST	REPEAT TITLE
Trials of Thomas Shaw (missing episode)	Once a Murderer
Will You Make a Bet with Death?	Bet with Death (missing episode)

Confused? Same Name, Different Story

Three titles were each used twice for *Suspense* episodes. They are often assumed to be repeat performances. The aviation story *Long Night* is one of the best performances of Frank Lovejoy in the series.

SAME TITLE...	... BUT A DIFFERENT STORY
End of the Road	• 1947-02-06 Car salesman falls in love with a wealthy man's wife, and then it gets strange and complicated • 1960-01-31 Marriage of a model and a violent ex-con; she seeks help of a district attorney
Long Night	• 1956-11-18 and 1958-07-13 An amateur aviator can't land his plane and is desperate for help from the control tower • 1960-01-10 Home invasion by an escaped psychopathic killer
Nightmare	• 1948-03-13 A man dreams he committed a murder, then realizes the murder was real. • 1949-09-01 Father seeks revenge over his son's death from a hit and run driver

Repeated Episodes

This is a list of the *Suspense* episodes that were repeated more than twice. Of course, *Sorry, Wrong Number* leads the list.

Eight times Sorry, Wrong Number

Four times
Night Reveals
Nobody Ever Quits/Night On Red Mountain
On a Country Road
Pit and the Pendulum
Wet Saturday (one of these repeats is half of an
    hour-long episode paired with *August Heat*)

Three times

Back for Christmas/Holiday Story
Backseat Driver
Banquo's Chair
The Black Curtain
Chicken Feed
Dead Ernest
The Diary of Sophronia Winters
Drive-In
Eve/Black Angel
A Friend to Alexander
Game Hunt
The Last Letter of Dr. Bronson
Life Ends at Midnight
Misfortune in Pearls /
    End of the String
Mr. Markham, Antique Dealer /
    Dealings of Mr. Markham
Murderous Revision /
    Murder on Mike
Neal Cream, Doctor of Poison /
    Story of Poison
Never Steal a Butcher's Wife /
    The Butcher's Wife
The Night Man
Occurrence at Owl Creek Bridge
Philomel Cottage
Rave Notice
Remember Me
The Signalman
Strange for a Killer
Suspicion
Too Hot to Live
The Treasure Chest of Don Jose
The Waxwork
Zero Hour

Suspense and *Escape* Shared Scripts

Escape was a CBS program that featured many classic stories and has always been held in high regard by collectors for the quality of its scripts and its production. The program did not feature Hollywood stars, like *Suspense* did, but it had the best talent in production and the best radio actors.

There has been a perception that *Escape* was not treated well by CBS executives because it never had a consistent time slot and was always being moved or canceled. On the other hand, the show is better viewed as a program that CBS could always rely on whenever there was unsponsored time in the schedule. The show was only briefly sponsored by ARCO Petroleum and spent most of its radio life as a sustained broadcast.

The series began in 1947 and ended in 1954. The use of classic stories or adapting recent novels and short stories meant that scriptwriting could be modestly budgeted. But that also meant writers who loved English literature could adapt stories they enjoyed on the printed page to radio. There is a spark of that writer's and actor's delight in many of the productions.

Most of the *Escape* production staff and actors worked on *Suspense* at one time or another. When *Escape* ended its run, the library of *Escape* scripts were always there for them to draw from when the shrinking *Suspense* budgets required less spending on original material. *Escape*'s scripts were well-written and could be produced with less time in planning and preparation because the production staff and performers were already familiar with them. Many of the *Escape* scripts had to be slightly abridged to comply with the shorter time slot that *Suspense* had in its later years.

TITLE	SUSPENSE	ESCAPE
Action	1953-10-05 Ben Wright	1948-04-04 Berry Kroeger 1949-07-21 Joseph Kearns
Back for Christmas	1943-12-23 Peter Lorre 1948-12-23 Herbert Marshall 1956-12-23 Herbert Marshall	1947-12-24 Paul Frees
Classified Secret	1955-11-22 Parley Baer	1953-04-12 Parley Baer
Command	1958-09-14 Elliott Reid	1949-12-06 Elliott Reid 1950-05-26 Harry Bartell
Country of the Blind	1957-10-27 Raymond Burr 1959-12-13 Bernard Grant	1947-11-26 William Conrad 1948-06-27 Paul Frees, Conrad 1949-03-20 Edmond O'Brien
Crossing Paris	1957-06-02 Hans Conreid	1950-08-25 Barney Phillips
Elementals	1960-06-12 Santos Ortega	1953-10-11 Tony Barrett
Flood on the Goodwins	1957-07-14 Herbert Marshall	1949-11-01 Jack Edwards 1954-07-24 Vic Perrin
I Saw Myself Running	1955-05-24 Charlotte Lawrence	1953-02-22 Georgia Ellis
I Won't Take a Minute (Suspense) Finger of Doom (Escape)	1945-12-06 Lee Bowman	1949-03-19 Ed Begley

TITLE	SUSPENSE	ESCAPE
Leinegen Versus the Ants	1957-08-25 William Conrad 1959-11-28 Luis Van Rooten	1948-01-14 William Conrad 1948-01-17 William Conrad 1948-05-23 William Conrad 1949-08-04 Tudor Owen
Lili and the Colonel	1955-05-17 Ramsay Hill	1953-05-03 Ben Wright
Lost Special	1943-09-30 Orson Welles	1949-02-12 Ben Wright
Man Who Liked Dickens	1947-10-09 Richard Ney	1952-12-21 Ramsay Hill
Man Who Stole the Bible	1956-11-25 John Lund	1950-05-05 Ben Wright 1951-08-30 Sam Pierce
Man Who Won the War	1958-09-07 Herbert Marshall	1950-02-28 John Dehner
Man Who Would be King	1959-05-31 Dan O'Herlihy	1947-07-07 Raymond Lawrence 1948-08-01 Ben Wright
Man with the Steel Teeth	1955-02-17 John Dehner	1953-03-15 Harry Bartell
Most Dangerous Game	1943-09-23 Orson Welles 1945-02-01 Joseph Cotten	1947-10-01 Hans Conreid
Occurrence at Owl Creek Bridge	1956-12-09 Victor Jory 1957-12-15 Joseph Cotten 1959-07-19 Vincent Price	1947-12-10 Harry Bartell

TITLE	SUSPENSE	ESCAPE
Outer Limit	1954-02-15 William Holden 1957-03-17 Frank Lovejoy	1950-02-07 Frank Lovejoy
Present Tense	1957-03-03 Vincent Price	1950-01-31 Vincent Price
Rim of Terror	1956-12-02 Barbara Whiting	1950-05-12 Nancy Kelly
Second Class Passenger	1957-01-20 Sterling Holloway	1949-07-28 Parley Baer
Shipment of Mute Fate	1957-01-06 Jack Kelly 1960-04-03 Bernard Grant	1947-10-15 Jack Webb 1948-03-28 Harry Bartell 1949-03-13 John Lund 1950-07-07 David Ellis
Sleeping Draught	1956-06-19 Ben Wright	1950-10-01 John Dodsworth 1953-04-05 Alex Harford
Study in Wax	1955-08-16 William Conrad	1953-02-01 William Conrad
Sundown	1958-05-04 Jackie Kelk	1950-06-23 Barton Yarborough
Sure Thing	1954-11-11 Hy Averback	1949-10-15 William Conrad 1950-01-17 Anthony Ross
The Cave	1955-12-20 Ben Wright	1950-12-24 John Dehner

TITLE	SUSPENSE	ESCAPE
The Game	1955-03-15 Sam Edwards	1953-08-30 Sam Edwards
The Island	1958-01-12 John Lund	1951-07-11 Harry Bartell 1953-03-08 Stacy Harris
Three Skeleton Key	1956-11-11 Vincent Price 1958-10-19 Vincent Price	1949-11-15 Elliott Reid 1950-03-17 Vincent Price 1953-08-09 Ben Wright
The Tramp	1956-07-25 Ben Wright	1953-03-01 Ben Wright
Two Came Back	1960-06-05 Bob Readick	1950-08-04 Stacy Harris
Vanishing Lady	1957-04-07 Vanessa Brown	1948-02-01 Joan Banks 1948-02-07 Joan Banks 1950-01-10 Del Castillo
Zero Hour	1955-04-05 Isa Ashdown 1958-05-18 Evelyn Rudie 1960-01-03 Francie Meyers	1953-10-04 Eve McVeagh

The Sad Case of John Garfield and the *Concerto for Killer and Eyewitnesses*

Actor John Garfield died a tragic, early death at age 39. Known for movie roles in *They Made Me a Criminal*, *Destination Tokyo*, *The Postman Always Rings Twice*, and his Oscar-nominated role in *Body and Soul*. He appeared on *Suspense* in 1945 (*Reprieve*) and in 1948 (*Death Sentence*) at a time of rising popularity.

He got caught up in the Communist scare in 1950, and testified before the House Committee on Un-American Activities. He refused to name Communist party members and said he knew none in the movie industry. He was listed in *Red Channels*. His reputation was damaged, though he did find ways to work, but not in the kind of properties that the trajectory of his career just a few years earlier would have deserved. Just prior to his death, he wrote an article "I Was a Sucker for a Left Hook," in reference to his movies about boxing, that he was duped by communist ideas and was staunchly against them. It was too late.

Garfield died of heart problems on May 21, 1952 at age 39. Many attributed his death to the stress of his career's challenges, especially friends who knew how troubled he was about it. He was diagnosed with heart problems a few years before, but heart imaging and diagnosis was primitive in the late 1940s compared to today's medical technology. It was not possible to know the full extent of his problems – doctors had to make educated guesses. We will never know the exact medical cause of his demise.

It is likely that some CBS execs did not want Garfield to appear on their programs during the peak of his public problems.

In October, 1950, Garfield was scheduled to record a script, *Concerto for Killer and Eyewitnesses*. This was early in the Elliott Lewis leadership of the series.

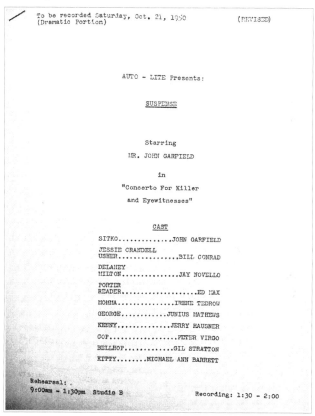

To be recorded Saturday, Oct. 21, 1950   (REVISED)
(Dramatic Portion)

AUTO - LITE Presents:

SUSPENSE

Starring

MR. JOHN GARFIELD

in

"Concerto For Killer
and Eyewitnesses"

CAST

SITKO..............JOHN GARFIELD
JESSIE CRANDELL
USHER...............BILL CONRAD
DELANEY
MILTON..............JAY NOVELLO
PORTER
READER....................ED MAX
MOMMA..............IRENE TEDROW
GEORGE...........JUNIUS MATHEWS
KENNY..............JERRY HAUSNER
COP..................PETER VIRGO
BELLHOP...........GIL STRATTON
KITTY.......MICHAEL ANN BARRETT

Rehearsal:
9:00am - 1:30pm Studio B   Recording: 1:30 - 2:00

We do not know if a Garfield's performance ever made it to the studio, and if it did, if it was recorded. We just know that it was scheduled for this particular day. Most recorded drama segments were broadcast anywhere from two to four weeks later. *Concerto* never made the schedule until after Garfield's death. This is the most clear case of a scheduled *Suspense* performance being impacted by *Red Channels*. All of the other instances that we have been able to find are murky or tenuous or only partially attributed.

At the time Garfield died, the *Suspense* schedule called for the season-ending performance of June 9, 1952 to be a reprise of *Sorry, Wrong Number*. There are many newspaper clippings to document this plan. Instead, later news items report that *SWN* would be moved to September, to start the show's new season.

It could be that Agnes Moorehead was not available for a June 9 performance, and that Lewis grabbed the unproduced *Concerto* script out of the files to fill in… or, Lewis facilitated the delay, seeing this as an opportunity to snub his nose in CBS bureaucracy who gave his friend, John Garfield, a hard time.

The decision was not a last-minute one, as *Concerto* is announced at the end of the June 2 performance of *A Good and Faithful Servant* with Jack Benny. Therefore, the decision to schedule *Concerto* was made before the *Servant* broadcast. It is interesting that *Concerto* is announced at the end of the show as "a story of revenge…" and that it would star Elliott Lewis, himself. Lewis may have been holding the script for Garfield for a time when the politics of his situation might improve.

The June 9 *Los Angeles Times* reported that *SWN* was originally planned for that night, but that…

> Producer-director Elliott Lewis adds a few new chores to his activities by starring in *Concerto for Killer and Eyewitnesses*. He'll do the show with earphones and toss cues to actors, musicians and sound effects men besides playing his part.

We will never know the full story, but the scheduling and performance of *Concerto* may have served multiple purposes for Lewis, to make CBS executives uncomfortable, and to pay homage to a maligned and departed friend.

The Robson Era

The William N. Robson era is a curious one, some of which can be summed up with the following in this question and answer:

> **Q**: What happens when you take a legendary and successful veteran radio producer, director, and writer and give them a show with no sponsor and an austere budget?
>
> **A**: One of the most interesting and entertaining periods of *Suspense*.

Bill Robson didn't have much to work with, but he squeezed every last bit of good radio drama out of a shrinking *Suspense* budget. He searched and located new radio scripts worth producing in a market where television was ravenous in its script consumption. He carefully selected scripts from the *Suspense* archives and those of other series that met the standard. He kept an ensemble cast of radio's best actors and production personnel together in compelling stories and scripts that they held in high regard and enjoyed. He probably had the constant threat of cancellation hanging over the franchise for the entire tenure. He preserved his budget with reused scripts, sometimes selected because of their small casts. He found himself relying on recorded music and many recorded effects.

The hardest cut was in music production, with no live orchestra. Robson navigated that limitation quite well. The Robson productions were solid, even if they were constrained by the eyeshade and sleeve protector pencil pushers of CBS who were throwing radio drama's pennies around like manhole covers.

There were more repeats in the Robson era than there were new scripts. Working in Robson's favor was that the audience for any kind of entertainment is always changing and changes over time. The people who listened in 1948 were not the same people in aggregate as those who were listening in 1953.

The technology was not really available yet for listeners to save their favorite programs. Home recording was still a luxury and very expensive. So if you wanted to hear that story "about the rats" or the one "about the ants" or "that woman who heard about the plot to commit murder because of crossed telephone lines," you had to wait and hope that it would be broadcast again. If the audience was able to hear a legendary *Escape* script on *Suspense* as a new presentation, that's a good thing.

NBC TV exec Pat Weaver was a pioneer in understanding this fact for that medium (probably his background in advertising) that the nature and size of an audience is affected by day, time slot, and competition. Even though something was broadcast at a particular time, there was still a large population that could not be in that audience but wanted to be. In that sense, *Suspense* reruns weren't a big deal. Just because of natural demographic patterns and media habits, the overwhelming majority of the Robson *Suspense* audience were new listeners. As collectors, we're more aware of the repeats because we can see all twenty years of its history at one time. It doesn't unfold to us a week at a time like it did for the listeners, or even for Robson. He was probably planning out eight to twelve weeks at a time very specifically, and then broad plans for everything else.

Robson kept *Suspense* on the air, and he did it with class. We wouldn't have had any new performances in the period unless he made good decisions, even about selection of the scripts that would be worth repeating.

The table below summarizes where the various scripts of the Robson years originated. Perhaps some title changes hide the identity of other scripts from series like *Romance*, and it is reasonable to believe that some scripts from *Modern Adventures of Casanova* (which Robson produced for Mutual, with Erroll Flynn starring) were used, but that series is not available.

The William N. Robson Years: A Tenure of Repeat Performances		
from previous episodes of...	**episodes**	**% of total**
Suspense	51	34.7%
Escape	19	12.9%
Romance	2	1.4%
On Stage	1	0.7%
Philip Morris Playhouse	1	0.7%
Modern Adventures of Casanova	1	0.7%
SUBTOTAL	**75**	**51.0%**
Original performances	**72**	**49.0%**
TOTAL	**147**	**100.0%**
revised June 16, 2019		

Robson was involved in the production of a series about the Cold War, *Operation Underground*. It aired from mid-1951 to mid-Spring 1952. It's not referenced often, and when it is, it's only in terms of how it affected the production and casting choices of *Gunsmoke*. It is suspected that some *Underground* scripts may have snuck into the *Suspense* canon. We already know a *The Man Behind the Gun* came in through the back door for a brief visit in *The Mission of the Betta*, and that was a Robson writing effort (under his Christopher Anthony pseudonym). Robson had great interest in the Cold War as a source of dramatizations. Today, *Operation Underground* still has no logs, no script resources, and no meaningful newspaper mentions. The audition program for *Operation Underground* is in circulation and is titled *Operation Danger*. None of the regular episodes are available.

The Missing Robson Era *Suspense* Openings

An enjoyable aspect of the Robson programs are his personal introductions to the episodes. *Suspense* had an "everybody's listening" approach before, but he acknowledged the individual listener. He spoke to that person directly, placing the upcoming story in context, becoming a little philosophical or historical, and then offering kind words for that week's lead performer. It's just me, the listener, and what Robson was offering.

These became such a part of the program that when the series moved to New York in 1959, when they would repeat scripts from his tenure, they repeated his introductions, too.

There are six *Suspense* episodes in circulation that are incomplete recordings and lack openings and closings. We don't have the chance to hear Robson's words. They are:

- 1957-01-03 Russian New Years
- 1957-05-19 Death and Miss Turner
- 1957-06-16 Trial by Jury
- 1958-03-30 The Sisters
- 1958-07-27 The Steel River Prison Break
- 1959-07-26 Night Man

The scripts for these episodes exist, so his words can be read. Perhaps actual recordings of these programs will be discovered and we can hear Robson utter his fine words. Until then, we'll have to imagine his voice as our eyes move across the pages.

1957-01-03 Russian New Years

Pawz Ve-ay-oo Snawveem Gawdawn. Happy New Year Russian style. Tonight in orthodox churches all over the world, high mass will be sung to usher in the new year according to the ancient Gregorian calendar. On this happy Russian holiday we take you back to another new year's eve more than a half-century ago to Moscow and the days when the serfs were ruled by Czars instead of commissars. Names and places have been changed to protect the innocent if any, but the facts are substantially the same today as they were then. so lay down *Das Kapital*, draw up a manifesto and listen as Helmut Dantine stars in "Russian New Years" -- a tale well calculated to keep you in... suspense.

(NOTE: The beginning of Robson's introduction is the phonetic spelling of the phrase so he would pronounce it correctly on air. С новым годом is the Cyrillic spelling of the three English words "Happy New Year.")

1957-05-19 Death and Miss Turner

We are truly honored to welcome back to our studio, one of America's finest actresses, and the first lady of suspense, Miss Agnes Moorehead. During the past 15 years, Miss Moorehead has lent her great talent to a score or more stories of suspense. She does so once again in the play specially written for her by William Spier. Listen then. Listen to Agnes Moorehead in "Death and Miss Turner" which begins in exactly one minute.

1957-06-16 Trial by Jury

Ever since Shakespeare wrote Portia's lines ---"The quality of mercy is not strained---" et cetera, mankind has been fascinated by lady lawyers. And why not? A forensic female is only putting her nascent capabilities to practical purposes --- but a lady criminal lawyer! A distaff mouthpiece! Such a one must indeed twice blesst, or in failure, thrice-cursed. so a one you will shortly meet as Miss Nancy Kelly stars in "Trial by Jury" which begins exactly one minute from now.

1958-03-30 The Sisters

Murder stories have fascinated man ever since Cain slew Abel. Perhaps because we can sublimate our own homicidal tendencies by revelling in how it was done and who done it. All too rarely do we find a murder story that concerns itself with why the deed was done. Such a one you are about to hear. And you are also about to hear the return from retirement of a great actress in her first radio role in many years, as Miss Frances Farmer stars as Lydia with Miss Cathy Lewis as Ellie in "The Sisters" which begins and exactly one minute.

1958-07-27 The Steel River Prison Break

If someone were to say to you that we are a nation of lawbreakers, you would probably break the law by committing assault and battery to prove he was wrong. Yet, our Pantheon is filled with scoundrels who have fondly made legendary heroes. Jesse James, Billy the Kid, John Dillinger ---. We weave an aura of glamour around the outlaws who had the intestinal fortitude to get away with it... and we secretly wish we had the same nerve. But, glamorous as it may seem, crime really doesn't pay, as we will attempt to prove in the morality play you are about to hear. Listen... listen, then, as Bartlett Robinson stars in "The Steel River Prison Break" which begins in just a moment---

1959-07-26 Night Man

Most of us, live out our lives in quiet desperation. Beset by nameless fears, plagued by unconscious guilts we adjust our neuroses to reality as best we may and somehow stay clear of the loony bin. Fortunate is he who knows what frightens him, for then he can do something about it – as does the young lady in the story you are about to hear – certainly there is nothing like action to dispel anxiety. And any psychiatrist can tell you that if you face up to your fear, it usually disappears – or does it? Listen. Listen then as Miss Marsha Hunt starts in "Night Man," which begins in just a moment –

Suspense *on Television*

Suspense was a highly rated television series, sponsored by Auto-Lite, for about five years. The shows were well done for their time from production and casting standpoints. A little over ten years ago, three sets of DVDs were released by Infinity Entertainment. They are no longer available. Used copies can be found on eBay and other sources. Sometimes the prices asked are very high, especially on Amazon. But if you are patient, you can occasionally get them for $20 to $30 per set. It's worth waiting for the price you want.

About 80+ episodes can be viewed on YouTube. I have created a public spreadsheet has lists them with links to the YouTube (or Archive.org) pages. https://docs.zoho.com/sheet/published.do?rid=bdalr35adaf4c726742faa22c153cfe7da531

There are 15 episodes based on radio scripts and are worth viewing just for comparison sake. They are:

Alibi Me	On a Country Road
Betrayal in Vienna	Photo Finish
Break-Up	Post Mortem
Dead Ernest	Remember Me?
Double Entry	Summer Storm
The Flame	The Tip
Help Wanted	Vidocq's Last Case
A Man in the House	

Dead Ernest is not as compelling on television as it was on radio. But other episodes are worth watching, especially to see how the stories are adapted to the small screen.

A Special Word to New OTR Collectors and Fans: Join in the Hunt!

New collectors with fresh ears and an attention to detail often detect curiosities that veteran collectors may miss. Some new collectors might feel intimidated by the experience of established collectors and feel they cannot make a contribution to the hobby or cannot have enough knowledge to do so. That's definitely not the case, as this research effort has shown.

Veteran collectors have already listened to the programs, years and perhaps decades ago. The fans usually focus on enjoying newly found material rather than going back to series and episodes they have already heard. This is the main reason why newer collectors can play a vital role in the documentation of this series and its recordings. New fans have fresh eyes and ears and often notice things others don't.

Can You Help in the Newspaper and Publication Research?

The advent of online archives of newspapers and industry magazines has helped provide insight into the series that would have required time-consuming and occasionally expensive on-site visits to libraries and archives. Now, these efforts can be done at any computer with Internet access. Sometimes researching the series can be just as engaging as a hobby as collecting and listening to the programs. Younger and new collectors are more familiar with new research tools and also practical computer use and file management. That means there are great opportunities for contributions that can enrich the OTR hobby.

One of the projects that is of great interest of this author is the finding and archiving of descriptive newspaper listings of all of the *Suspense* broadcasts. The main focus in this project is finding missing episodes, of course, but the entire series can benefit from this research.

Because of the time lag in publishing between the information sent to newspapers in advance of the actual broadcasts, one can find cast changes and episode changes that are often quite interesting and reveal much about the show's production.

Suspense, like any other program, was subject to pre-emption by major news events, especially during WW2. That information can be fascinating, adding more insights to show history.

It has become evident from researching other series that *Suspense* was followed in newspaper listings in great detail longer than other programs. *Yours Truly, Johnny Dollar* shared the last two years of network drama together. Newspaper editors rarely allocated page space to the descriptions of *YTJD* programs. It's easy to understand their reasoning, though OTR fans may disagree: *YTJD* was a formula show, and every week Johnny investigated, was misled, shot at or otherwise in danger, and then solved the crime. *Suspense*, on the other had, was an anthology and featured different actors in lead roles every week. Editors likely believed readers were more interested in that kind of series. The editorial decisions varied from newspaper to newspaper, with each editor selecting the details they believed were right for their audiences.

The other important aspect of the research is even more basic: listening to the shows!

Help by Listening to the Shows!

Though it seems strange to suggest this, *Suspense* recordings are not documented as well as commonly assumed.

As noted in this book, *Suspense* is probably the most-recorded radio series in terms of the numbers of different types of recordings. There are still east-west programs that have not been properly identified, and the variety of AFRS recordings have never been cataloged well. Cast listings need to be verified and expanded. There are recordings with dialogue and advertising differences that have not been documented with precision.

Join Us, Won't You?

That's the closing comment of *Johnny Dollar* after he teases the next week's program, but it fits just as well here. And in the process of helping out… you get to listen to "radio's outstanding theater of thrills"! Combining the research and listing increases the enjoyment of the series greatly.

Find your fellow fans at the Cobalt Club (my forum name is "Greybelt"), at the Old Time Radio Researchers page on Facebook, or by emailing me at suspenseOTR@gmail.com.

Cobalt Club OTR Forum membership is free, and many collectors use the forum to research shows and the radio era and also to post high quality recordings of all types of golden age shows. Many of us in this *Suspense* effort are there. http://cobaltclubannex.forumotion.com

About the Author

Joseph W. Webb, Ph.D.
3650 Rogers Rd. #275, Wake Forest, NC 27587 USA
E-mail: suspenseOTR@gmail.com

I first heard OTR on jazz station WRVR-FM in NYC when they were rebroadcasting Charles Michelson syndications of *The Shadow* in 1972. Eventually I stumbled into the bigger hobby and Jay Hickerson's *Hello Again* newsletter. I began trading with collectors around the US, and with the help of others got into the process of finding new material. I started collecting on cassettes and then I made the "big boy" move to reel-to-reel with a Sony TC-250 (thank you, Santa!).

I used to enjoy buying recordings from Rex Bills' *Golden Age Radio* and early OTR collector Don Maris, among others. Through trading, I become one of the hobby's more active collectors. My OTR activities through my college years were financed by being an OTR dealer (*Old Radio Warehouse, Nostalgia Warehouse)* especially for the sale of OTR books and OTR fan publications). I got involved in the Friends of Old Time Radio conventions from 1976 to about 1984 before and then pursued academic and career interests and family life.

The fanzine *Collector's Corner* was published by me with Bob Burnham with the help of Bob Burchett in the late '70s and early '80s. Earlier, I had worked on *Airwaves* with collector Jerry Chapman.

In the early 2000s I came back into the hobby and found a thriving digital recording collector community. I was disappointed by the sound quality of series that I had originated into circulation years before. I had my original disc dub tapes encoded by a sympathetic new collector. Thus began my second OTR journey!

In my "second time around" of collecting, I have many new friends devoted to the history and preservation of those golden age of radio dramas. It's been great fun to be back in the hobby as an empty-nester and retiree with more time and resources to devote to its pursuit. One of the great pleasures of second phase has been getting in contact with the 1970s and 1980s collectors I knew who are still active. I have also tried to contact inactive collectors from those years to introduce them to the digital OTR hobby of today and cultivate their interest once more.

My research websites

There is a special website where I am posting new information about *Suspense* as I find it. Go to https://sites.google.com/view/suspense-collectors-companion and check it out.

Another series I have found interesting is *The Big Story*. It adapted many news stories but dramatized them with disguised names and circumstances. This site finds the news stories behind the scripts that inspired *The Big Story* episodes.

Made in the USA
Lexington, KY
24 June 2019